HE TOUCHED ME

He Touched Me

Conversion Stories of
NORMAN VINCENT PEALE,
BRUCE LARSON, ERNEST GORDON,
BILL WILSON & OTHERS

IRVING HARRIS

ABINGDON PRESS
NASHVILLE

HE TOUCHED ME

Copyright © 1985 by Abingdon Press

Library of Congress Cataloging in Publication Data

Main entry under title:
He touched me.

1. Converts—Biography. I. Peale, Norman Vincent, 1898- . II. Harris, Irving.
BV4930.H38   1985   248.2'4'0922 [B]   84-20365

ISBN 0-687-16680-2

MANUFACTURED BY THE PARTHENON PRESS AT
NASHVILLE, TENNESSEE, UNITED STATES OF AMERICA

TO

JULIA CRAWFORD HARRIS

loving wife and faithful teammate

without whom

this book would not have been written

And to this day nothing is so persuasive to our hearts as just the story of a personal experience in religion.

—ALEXANDER WHYTE

CONTENTS

Author's Foreword   9

1. The Big Switch   11
   MARGARET AUSTIN

2. This Is My Story   19
   BY NORMAN VINCENT PEALE

3. My Personal Treasure Hunt   25
   BY BRUCE LARSON

4. A Victim of Grace   34
   BY ERNEST GORDON

5. Sand in the Gears   44
   JACK ROWLES

6. Freedom from Fear   50
   JAMES BELL NICOLL, M.D.

7. The Turning Point   56
   KAY LIMBURG

8. Four Steps to a New Life   63
   BY IRVING HARRIS

9. Into and Out of a Million Dollars   78
    MILLARD FULLER

10. The Story of A.A.'s Bill Wilson   87
    BY IRVING HARRIS

11. Disinherited   104
    ALYS BOROSS SMITH

12. A Jewish Businessman Discovers   112
    the Messiah
    JOSEPH KLUTCH

13. Walking in the Light   117
    BY NORMAN GRUBB

14. A Special Collection of Stories   123
    HELEN SHOEMAKER AND OTHERS

15. Toward a Fuller Life   140
    BY WILLIAM POPE

    Epilogue   153
    BY SAMUEL M. SHOEMAKER

The most thrilling experience in life is to feel in vital touch with the Living God. He is our answer to fear and frustration, to lack of purpose and bad habits. His forgiveness and his presence spell freedom and joy.

There are many excellent books to help us grow deeper in our faith and in our understanding of God, but not many current authors tell us how to make the initial contact with him. Just as a baby has to be born before it can be nurtured, so you and I need a new birth before we can truly understand the *full* meaning of Christian faith.

In this book I have focused on the experience of conversion—the starting point of our basic relationship with God. Conversion is not the whole story, but it is the real beginning of the new life.

As the stories in this book reveal, conversion happens to different people in different ways. Some find the new life suddenly, with their outlook and nature changed almost overnight. Many like myself, however, experience conversion more gradually, often in a succession of steps. As described in chapter 8, I took four separate steps before I felt possessed of a quality of life that made me defenseless and enabled me to communicate faith effectively to other people.

The men and women whom you will meet in these stories have all been my friends. Some I met when I was working as editor of *The Evangel*, a magazine published at Calvary House, 61 Gramercy Park, New York, during the late Samuel M. Shoemaker's rectorship of the church there. This magazine won widespread interest in the United States and in Canada and even touched people in well over a hundred nations around the world. When Sam Shoemaker was called to another church in Pittsburgh, the magazine was incorporated as Faith at Work and moved uptown to offices at 8 West 40th Street, just opposite the New York Public Library. With Faith at Work, Inc., there developed an ever increasing number of weekend conferences in various parts of the country; for, under God, we found ourselves spearheading a lay person's small-group movement.

As you read, it will become clear that a new life is available to everyone, but it is only realized as you deliberately turn toward the Source and make a conscious choice to accept what God offers you. It is like a watershed beyond which lies a new country with fresh opportunities and happier prospects. In this land, as Robert Browning once put it, "The best is yet to be."

—Irving Harris

7 Cleveland Lane
Princeton, New Jersey

CHAPTER ONE

The Big Switch

MARGARET AUSTIN

How does one switch from a non-Christian basis of life to the Christian way? Here is one woman's story, a blow-by-blow account of what happened to an American homemaker.

Margaret Austin ended up working as a court reporter in Houston, Texas. She had been baptized and married by Christian rites. With two children, daughters by a man who later divorced her, she hadn't darkened the door of a church for fourteen years, nor did she ever intend to go to church again. She was vaguely aware that there was something in the universe besides people, but that this being was even remotely concerned with individuals like herself seemed presumptuous and unrealistic. She thought that anyone who held such a philosophy must have a hole in his head.

A vague duty to expose her children to a Christian Sunday school sent her shopping around a bit, but the churches she visited, while "nice," seemed oh so dull!

Then one of her children had a birthday and wished to invite a special friend from school to a party. Margaret looked up the friend's father's name in the telephone book only to find a "Rev." in front of it. "Oh, no," she thought, "I can't get mixed up with a preacher's family." However, in the long run, her daughter wanted the friend so badly that Margaret screwed up her courage and made the call. It turned out that there were four children in the preacher's family and when the day arrived they *all* came—plus the mother.

The hostess acted warily, but—to her surprise—the preacher's wife was attractive and seemed to have a lot of zip. In spite of herself, Margaret enjoyed the party, so much so that when the guests were leaving, she told the preacher's wife, if her husband ever wanted to tangle with a thoroughgoing agnostic, to send him over. Secretly Margaret believed she was smart enough to confound him easily.

Now the preacher was Claxton Monro, at that time rector of St. Stephen's Church in Houston. He and his wife, Vicky, had both been agnostics, too, so they well knew what it was like to believe in not much of anything. They knew the questions about religion that plagued people like Margaret, and they also knew some of the answers. As opportunity offered, they gently spoon-fed our agnostic friend with simple Christian truths and eventually led her to a service at St. Stephen's Church.

That first service, she reports, was a most unhappy experience. Margaret believed practically nothing of what she heard; and she could not, in all honesty, even join in the prayers. She spent the hour mute, angry, and rebellious, wondering how the St. Stephen's staff could teach such unrealistic nonsense to children, much less expect grown-ups to swallow it. When the service was over, she couldn't get out of the church fast enough, only afraid that someone she knew would see her and think she had flipped.

But Vicky Monro called that afternoon. She had little to say about the church, but she gave a compelling description about another kind of a service, the first of which was to be held that very evening. Lay people, she said, were going to talk about what God had done for them personally in their own lives. Would Margaret like to come? The invitation was without pressure, and the critical mother felt free to accept or not. Well, she went and for two reasons: what small faith she did have was based on people, and, further, she very much liked Clax and Vicky Monro.

That night Clax began the service by saying that he believed the lay ministry was being badly neglected in the church generally. Sunday evenings at St. Stephen's, he added, were now to provide an opportunity to rectify this by having a program with a number of lay people speaking on what faith had come to mean to them personally. As a starter he told his own story and what it was that had brought him into the ministry. Margaret Austin found it fascinating to hear how, as a graduate of M.I.T., well-launched in his career of an engineer, he had made the change, but as an agnostic she had her defenses up, insisting within herself that Clax could only tell such a story because he was a minister. She decided that nothing similar could ever happen to an ordinary person like herself.

However, Margaret returned to the church and attended both the morning and evening services for the next several weeks. In these services she heard

13

lawyers, writers, salesmen, and housewives. While she determined not to believe much that was said, there was no question but that she greatly liked the speakers, and she had to admit that they had qualities she had rarely seen before. They seemed utterly sincere, all of them, and they radiated a sense of well-being, even of happiness. As a businesswoman she hadn't seen anyone truly happy in years and had come to think that happiness was limited to the very young and to idiots.

Besides this, she heard laughter—wonderful, full-bodied laughter. Furthermore, there was a glow on the faces of the speakers, and our cynic couldn't help wondering where it came from. After a while she began to want some of the glow for herself. The clincher came when she saw married couples looking at each other as if they really *liked* each other. That was definitely an unexpected shock.

After three months she finally went to Clax Monro and told him that, while she couldn't buy this thing called Christianity, she wanted to try it anyway! She asked what she should do to live a God-centered life when she didn't believe in God. She was sure he'd load her with good advice and urge her to consecrate herself. Not at all. He just told her to experiment—to act as if she thought God existed and see if it worked. He also suggested that she read something of a spiritual nature every day.

His advice sounded awfully dull, but she was relieved and she went ahead. She had also been told to pray, so she started on this. At first she prayed "gimme" prayers—nothing but these at first. Gimme this, gimme that. And all these prayers were said as she lay flat on her back.

But she soon realized that gimme prayers were children's prayers and that if she was going to give her spiritual experiment a fair shake, she would have to put some real zeal into it and really work at it.

Feeling ridiculous and knowing it couldn't possibly pan out, she proceeded with her first sincere experiment. This was a dilly. She purposely chose her most difficult problem ever—her years-old hatred for a certain person. It was a deep, full-blown hate and one she believed was perfectly justified. Her project was to get rid of that feeling.

This initial experiment was coupled with her first kneeling prayer, the very first one she had engaged in since childhood. To get on her knees and bow her head was in itself a tough exercise; she was a proud woman and not in the habit of bowing her head to anyone. The combination of kneeling and praying for someone she hated proved a sweat-provoking ordeal. She tried over and over again to say a prayer—even a short one—for the person concerned and to wish him well, but that first morning she completely failed. She couldn't whisk even a tiny prayer through her head, not one.

However, the next day she finally triumphed. First she was gripped by the persistent thought that God couldn't be expected to remove personal hatred. Then she thought she had better continue trying, and that evening, with much agony of soul, she was finally able to slide through her botched-up brain one small prayer—a prayer consisting of a brief but sincere good wish for this hated person. She sent her prayer through to a God in whom she still didn't really believe and asked Him to send it on. The whole procedure was as hard as cutting off an arm with a small knife, but she did it.

Then, by the third night, the whole business had become a personal challenge. She wondered if she could do it again. Once more she knelt down and, miraculous to say, she articulated an almost presentable prayer for the hated one. And at that same moment God lifted an incredible burden off her shoulders. She went to bed and slept like a child.

The effect of this experience lasted, and she began to catch a glimmer of the freedom practicing Christians have—freedom from guilt as well as from hate, and freedom from anxiety and from fear.

Of course, evil never sleeps, and her rational mind began sawing away, coming up with the idea that what she had done was simply good psychology. Think well of a person, and one simply can't hate him. So, unbeliever that she still was, she decided that she had simply done what was psychologically very sound. What a relief not to give God the credit!

Then she tried another experiment. She called this one "peace in the home." Although she hadn't realized it, as a non-Christian she had been utterly selfish, especially at home, and domineering with her children. She considered herself just fine—"peachy-keen," in fact, clever, smart, and really quite a person. But her inside didn't match the outside. At this point God gave her the insight to realize that she wasn't what she ought to be but that all was not lost. Unexpectedly, she came to realize that *with His help* she could become a better person. So she prayed for a personal change, as well as for peace in the home, and asked that she might become different—more loving, kinder, and more just. She prayed especially that she might remember that her daughters were God's children as well as hers.

At first any difference in the home was most nebulous and erratic—but so were her prayers. Nevertheless, whenever she remembered to pray a "good, honest prayer," the change in her home's atmosphere became immeasurably better. For a while she insisted that the improvement was merely coincidence, but there came a point beyond which "coincidence" was clearly a misnomer. It didn't fit. God had to be working. There was no other adequate explanation.

Then Margaret decided to make one more test—this would be the clincher. It had to do with tithing, a subject that had been frequently mentioned at St. Stephen's, mentioned so often that she had concluded it might be the real reason that she was urged to attend church. The staff wanted her money. Deep down, she knew this wasn't really so, but anyway there was the possibility.

When she made out her first tithing card she says that she nearly died. Everything within her rebelled: the money was hers—she had made it—and if a big hunk of it went down the drain, she would never be able to pay her bills.

But as with everything else in her new life, things didn't work out that way. Quite the contrary:

—she had enough money to cover everything;
—besides, her desire for material things subtly changed;
—money went further, for some of the things she had thought she needed proved unessential;
—then she also lost her deep-seated fear that she wouldn't make enough to go around;

—and best of all, she lost her intense interest in money as such.

To sum up, while money had previously formed a kind of golden dream of a never-never land where it and happiness were synonymous, she was now finding happiness without money. The tithing check, strangely, became the one check she most enjoyed writing.

One day Margaret turned into the driveway of her house and had an experience that topped everything else. She had thus far always been one to live in the future: six months from now, she used to think, everything would be different—meaning better. But that day a brand-new thought came to her. It was this: "Nothing has changed—same house, same job, same children—yet everything is different from what it was when I began to be a Christian." She realized that, in a remarkable way, happiness and peace marked a life previously torn by discord, wishful thinking, and considerable unhappiness. As she sat a moment in the car she further thought, "This is it. This is my life, and by the grace of God I will learn to live within its limitations and have a productive, happy, and even joyful existence."

And this she says she does "with a singing heart."

CHAPTER TWO

This Is My Story

BY NORMAN VINCENT PEALE

My father was a preacher. He served in Cincinnati and in areas round about. When I was a little boy, Father was pastor of what was known as a circuit, five rural churches.

One of the greatest things—perhaps the greatest thing—that ever happened to me occurred in one of those little churches as I sat there one night with my mother. They were holding what were called "protracted meetings"—several meetings that went on for a lengthy time in the winter season.

Dave Henderson was a man in the community, a big fellow, and he was mean. Profane, a drunkard, foul-mouthed, he was known all around the country-side as a tough guy, but he always came to the revival meetings. He would weep and he would sing, but they said in that community that not even God Himself could save Dave.

Then one night when my father gave the invitation to accept Christ, it seemed as though the building shook as a tremendous man walked down the aisle. I turned around, and my mother said, "Glory to God, it's Dave Henderson." He came to the altar and knelt, and people gathered around him and "prayed him through."

I can remember him yet, though I was very young at that time. Dave stood up, raised his arms, and said, "Glory to God! I'm saved!" And he was, too, for he lived in that community for another fifty years, and when he died he was by common consent the greatest saint in all the countryside round about.

Well, the next night I asked my mother and father if I could "go forward," and that was the night I found Jesus Christ. But I'm a tough case, and I had to be saved several times! I believe it is perfectly possible for a person to be saved once and for all, but let me tell you that human nature is bad, and the devil is very powerful, and he can get into the mind of anyone who does not have the Spirit in power to ward him off.

But to get back to my father. He was a real person—a forthright, honest, dedicated man. I've had good fortune and been favored, but for my father, year in and year out for the eighty-five years of his life, there were only Jesus Christ and people. He had only one message: that Jesus Christ could save you from sin, that Jesus Christ could change your life, that Jesus Christ could do anything for you.

He was a medical doctor before he became a minister, and I was brought up on a combination of medicine and religion. Heal men's bodies—heal their souls—heal the whole man. When I finally got to working with psychology in my ministry, Father said that it could be used to the glory of God "if you didn't go too far with it"—which I hope I haven't.

Once when I was in theological seminary and bursting with "intellectuality," I came home. My father, then Superintendent of Churches, asked me to preach at a little country church one Sunday when the minister was either sick or away. Father said, "Now remember it's just a simple country church—just farmer people—and don't think you're so smart because you've been to a theological school in Boston!"

All week long I worked on that sermon, and it was heavily packed with theology, as I understood it at the time. On Saturday I sat down again with my father. He always sat in a rocking chair with his feet on a railing, and this time he said, "Read me that sermon." So I read it to him, and when I was through he just sat there rocking.

Finally he asked, "Norman, you want to know what I think you ought to do with that sermon?"

I said, "Yes, Dad, tell me."

He said: "Go out and burn it! In the first place, you wrote it all out. Get rid of the manuscript. Never read a sermon. If you don't feel it in your soul, so that you're burning to tell it, then you shouldn't preach it. If you have to depend upon a manuscript, you'll never get anywhere with it. Go out back and burn it."

Then he went on: "Listen. You found Jesus Christ, didn't you? He helped you overcome your sins, your weaknesses, your inferiority complex. Well, you must go out there in the morning and tell the people about Jesus, and don't talk theoretically—just tell them about Him as you personally know Him."

"But I can't make that last twenty-five minutes," I said.

"Then let it go at five," he said. "The important thing is not how long you preach, but what you say."

21

So I went the next day to a beautiful little church at the corner of two Ohio cornfields. The corn was knee-high, so it must have been around the Fourth of July. It was one of those sweet-smelling Sundays, peaceful, clear-washed, and quiet. I went into the pulpit to see if everything was all right, and then the people began to come in—the girls all spic and span, starched up like they used to be, pink ribbons, yellow ribbons; the boys sort of abashed, the families all strung out in the pews with father at one end and mother at the other to properly police the children.

They were fine-looking people, the salt of the earth, and I stood up to tell them about Jesus Christ.

I'm sure you have experienced how once in a while, under the power of the Holy Spirit, you get a deep silence in a church, deep but very much alive, as though something great trembles in the air. It happened that morning: the misty look in people's eyes, the expression of longing in their faces. That experience taught me that Jesus Christ is where the people meet.

After the sermon was over I was invited for dinner by some of the folks from that congregation, and a big, heavy-set man came out on the porch to talk to me. He sat down, slapped me on the knee, and began, "Son, you know you've got a powerful lot to learn about preaching, don't you?"

"Yes, sir," I said, "I know that."

"But," he said, "you've got a couple of things right, and the main one is you talked only about Jesus. The second thing is that you talked to people in their own language so that everybody could understand. Just keep doing that—talk in simple language and talk about Jesus, for Jesus is wonderful."

Well, since then I've gone all up and down the land, and I honestly believe that deep down in people's hearts there are love and faith in Jesus Christ. God help us, most of us aren't very faithful to Him, but still we know He is the answer. That has been my spiritual experience.

I also believe that the Bible is the inspired word of God, and I've never found a case where the Bible doesn't work. The older I get and the more difficulties I have to face with myself and with other people, the more I know that the old, basic, fundamental principles of the Christian religion are abundantly right and sound.

The Virgin Birth, the Resurrection, the Holy Spirit—I believe in them all. I believe in the Cross. I have believed in the Cross all my life and have preached that salvation is at the foot of the Cross.

Over the years what I have tried to do in my simple way is to preach the gospel, the old, Christ-centered, church-centered, Holy Spirit-centered gospel. Perhaps I've used a new kind of terminology, but I believe you've got to reach people on their own knowledge-level where they understand, and I think the average American is not educated in the terminology of the church as people were years ago.

I know a man named Charlie who had many problems. Every time I tried to make suggestions to help him, he would reply, "I have half-a-mind to do that."

Finally, it came to me to say: "Charlie, I believe your trouble is that you are a 'half-a-minder.' You're always telling me you have half-a-mind to do something. You'd like to be strong in your morals and in your faith, and you'd like to be effective in your

23

business. But let me tell you, you'll never in the world reach any of those goals unless you go *all* out instead of *half* out."

He asked, "How can one really get changed?"

Well, I had been doing my best to change this man and was baffled. But just then someone began to play a hymn on a nearby carillon, and the sound floated in at the window. I got up and walked over to look out, and across the way was a church with an illuminated cross on its steeple.

I said: "Come over here, Charlie. Did you ever hear about the Cross when you were a boy and went to church? Haven't you heard that Jesus Christ hung on the Cross for the remission of sins and that you can be saved by faith in the Savior who gave his life on the Cross for you?"

The strangest look came over Charlie's face, and at once he fell to his knees and surrendered his life to the Lord Jesus Christ. He was transformed before my very eyes!

I had applied my theological knowledge and psychological insight to him for two years—and I won't write that off completely, because at least the idea of "half-a-mind to" has some psychological power, but at any rate, it wasn't psychology that saved Charlie. It was the Lord Jesus Christ.

This is my story.

CHAPTER THREE

My *Personal Treasure Hunt*

BY BRUCE LARSON

M y own personal treasure hunt began as far back as I can remember. One of my first clues was an overriding feeling of loneliness. As a matter of fact this feeling is one of my earliest memories. My awareness of loneliness took a different shape in every phase of my growing up. But it was always there. When I was very young I dreamed often that my parents had died, leaving me all alone. You see, they were my only family. I was the solitary child of a couple who were old when I was born. My father was sixty and my mother was forty. They had separately immigrated from London and met and married in Chicago. In both cases, they were the only members of the family to come to America. So I had no grandparents, no uncles or aunts, or brothers or sisters. If my parents died, I would truly be all alone. I can still remember all the details of the recurring

Bruce Larson is currently pastor of the University Presbyterian Church of Seattle, Washington. Prolific writer and popular speaker, he was formerly the president of Faith at Work, Inc. This story is taken from the book *The Passionate People* by Keith Miller and Bruce Larson, with permission of Word Books, Publisher, Waco, Texas, 1979.

nightmares in which I attended their joint funeral. . . . and was left all alone in the world.

When I was four the stock market crashed. From that day until he died, my father's business was in grave financial difficulty. The sheriff was always lurking in the shadows, about to put a padlock on a bankrupt laundry. The practical implications of this were that we moved literally every two years, looking for cheaper housing. All through my growing-up years I was the new boy in the neighborhood—the last one chosen for sandlot ball and the first dropped from the guest list of birthday parties when the list was getting too big. All through those lonely years I can remember wanting more than anything to belong to a gang—*my* gang. I didn't even want to be the leader of the gang—just an indispensable member of it.

On my thirteenth birthday we had just moved to a new town. We were living in two rooms of a rundown apartment hotel. My mother planned the party and cooked my favorite meal, roast pork stuffed with prunes and apples (a Swedish specialty), and invited about a dozen people—none of whom was under seventy. So began my teenage years.

Then the shape of loneliness took on romantic overtones. I was in love with love and desperately wished I had some girl who cared about me. I have indelible memories of sitting in my room doing homework by the open window on the first warm days of spring. They were unbelievably bright after a harsh Illinois winter. The warm winds rustled the forsythia bushes and made the lilac buds nod. I pictured what it might be like to walk down the street in the springtime holding some special girl's hand. My constant yearning for someone to love who would love me back kept me in turmoil.

I guess I was not very negotiable because the girls I wanted never wanted me. By the time I was in high school we had moved to an affluent Chicago suburb. The trouble was that we lived in the low-rent district. My clothes were usually too small and not very sharp to begin with. The family car was old—no competition for my friends' classy new models. And, what was worse, I had never learned to jitterbug. In those days only social lepers couldn't dance the "Lindy." No wonder my stock was low.

While I was in high school, America entered World War II. I proudly served as a junior air raid warden and an assistant block captain. I enthusiastically bought war bonds. By that time I was earning my own money with afterschool jobs and summer employment, picking crops or working in the oil fields. One season I managed the lunch counter of the local Walgreen's and brought home the impressive salary of eighteen dollars a week.

As the war continued, propaganda films proliferated and my own sense of outrage grew. Most of all I wanted to do something about the destruction of millions of Jews. At seventeen, in a burst of patriotism and against the wishes and advice of parents and friends, I enlisted in the army.

Although I didn't see it at the time, the connection between the lonely boy who so much wanted to belong and the impetuous idealist who wanted to do something about wars and atrocities seems obvious now. Since I have become a Christian, I understand that God had placed in me, as I think He does in all of us, in varying degrees, a deep hunger to belong and a great desire to help people who cannot help themselves. These were the two clues in my personal treasure hunt of life.

My disillusionment with the army life-style was instantaneous and almost total. But one of the great serendipities for me was finding a family. Without knowing it, I had been looking for many years for the Fourth Platoon of I Company, 397th Infantry Regiment. Those thirty men who trained together and ultimately went overseas to fight in France and Germany became a caring, fighting, drinking, singing, lending family. We alternately loved and hated each other—just like a real family. As much as I despised army life, I felt that in some strange way I had come home.

While we were still training at Fort Bragg, North Carolina, my father had surgery. The Red Cross arranged an emergency furlough, and I sat up all night on a dirty train as it clanked through the Midwest to Chicago, desperately hoping that my father would not die. I arrived with the dawn only to learn that he had died a few hours before. I think I wept without interruption for twenty-four hours. And, though I loved my father, my tears were not for him, but for my own loneliness at losing him.

On the day before the funeral, an enormous box of roses arrived with a card that said "Our love and sympathy. The Fourth Platoon." In that moment the biblical phrase, "The Lord giveth and the Lord taketh away" was especially applicable. In this case, the Lord had taken away my dad—and given me—a *family!*

It was a whole year before my old nemesis— "loneliness"—caught up with me again, and I will never forget that awful night. It was during the last winter of the war. Our division was on the line, fighting in the Vosges Mountains in Alsace-Lorraine, an area between France and Germany proper. Due to some tactical error, our company managed to move ahead of the rest of the regiment and nightfall found us on a wooded hillside without food or blankets, surrounded by the enemy. The plan was to dig in, spend the night and try to fight our way back to friendly lines at dawn.

The enemy had other plans. They knew and understood our position. We were the proverbial fish in the barrel, and they commenced to shoot at us with timed-fire artillery. Shells exploded in the air and released great showers of shrapnel into open foxholes. It was a horrifying, eerie night, full of manmade lightning and thunder. Branches of trees rained down upon us with each shell burst.

I was sharing a foxhole with a new replacement named Riley who had been assigned to my squad just the day before. Sometime past midnight a large piece of shrapnel found its mark in Riley's midsection. I tried to treat him with our first-aid kits but there was too little for too much. I crawled over to a neighboring hole to fetch our company medic, but it did not take him long to see that Riley was beyond his skills. We'd need to get him to the battalion aid-station if he was to have a chance of making it. The medic administered a shot of morphine and went back to his own foxhole.

As a squad leader, I was responsible for getting Riley back to the aid-station. I spent most of that night crawling from foxhole to foxhole looking for a volunteer to help me carry the litter. No one had ever heard of Riley. And no one would volunteer. Through my anger, tears, and fear I had to admit that I wouldn't have volunteered either had it not been my responsibility or one of my best friends. I crawled back to the foxhole, held Riley in my arms, and felt him die with the coming of dawn.

I never felt so alone in my life. I sobbed for Riley and for his wife and children whose pictures he had proudly displayed the day before. But I knew somehow that my tears were also for my father and his death and the loneliness I still felt. Perhaps most of all I sobbed for me and my fresh awareness that when the chips were down, I would probably be as alone and friendless as Riley had been. My dream of a caring family—of belonging—was shattered. In the cold light of that dawn I grew up. I became a man in one night, which is to say that I became a cynic. I had come full circle. The lonely little boy had become a lonely grown man—who would never trust anyone again.

Months passed. The war ended. Occupation began, and with it dullness, boredom, and moral stagnation. I felt that I was swimming in a sea of garbage. Even worse, the garbage was inside of me. But that was evidently the prologue for God's next act in my life.

For God had a witness in our midst all through the years of training, fighting, and occupation. He was our regimental chaplain. He was anything but relational and did not make friends easily. He was sober, serious, sincere, and wore his Victorian morality like an unyielding suit of shining armor. He publicly denounced the things he saw most of us doing every day. He was not someone you would easily confide in and probably the last person with whom you'd choose to be marooned on a desert island. But (and I will never cease to be thankful for that "but") he was a man who had a personal relationship with Jesus Christ and spoke about it convincingly. And as unattractive as I felt him to be, this man's faith did make him different in a positive way from the rest of us. Many of us were church members who believed that someone called Jesus Christ had died for our sins. But the chaplain was someone who had a day-to-day relationship with Him. And because of that one life in our midst, God showed me during those months that there are two very different ways to live—for and by yourself or for and with Him.

One night I was standing guard in a bombed-out building on the hills surrounding Stuttgart. I was fed up with myself and ashamed that I had taken on the coloration of the social and moral garbage of my surroundings. More than that, I began to sense that the dream each of us shared, to return home to normalcy, was in fact nothing but a dream. Returning to loved ones, jobs, careers, schools would not really change us. What I was now in Stuttgart I would always be, unless I opted for the alternative I saw before me. My overseas environment had not made me what I was. It simply revealed what I always had been and always would be. There was no veneer. The future was uncertain. But clearly the choice was mine.

I took my carbine off my shoulder and laid it against a brick wall, ground out my cigarette, knelt down and looked up at the stars in the night sky through the charred rafters of the building. I prayed my first real prayer, "Lord, if you really are there, and, if you really do love me and want me, please come in and take over my life."

During the days and weeks which followed, quiet miracles took place—of morality and cleansing, of changed values and goals. I seemed to have new eyes to see and new ears to hear. But at first I told no one for fear that I was on a trip that wasn't genuine or would not last. But it was real and it did last and has continued to this very day. That is not to say that there are not days when the whole adventure of faith does not seem unreal—or when for my own convenience I wish it were all a lie. But the relationship to Jesus Christ that I saw in one hardshell Baptist infantry chaplain has become the central reality of my life.

Eventually the army sent me home. And Chicago seemed very different. In those early months as a new civilian I can remember vividly walking the streets in the Loop and on the near Northside and feeling a great sense of love for every person who walked beside me or crossed my path. I felt as if I knew the ultimate secret about life—that God loves us and cares about us and has forgiven us—that Jesus Christ wants to live in us and with us and share our lives.

I can remember feeling very special because of this secret. It was as if a shaft of powerful light followed me wherever I went. I was both delighted and embarrassed by the sensation of walking in a shaft of light. As self-centered as it seemed, it was nevertheless real and powerful. Years later I discovered that Hannah Whitall Smith in her classic book, *The Christian's Secret of a Happy Life*, had a similar experience.

As I walked the streets, I looked strangers in the eye and ached for them to know and share the secret. I must have prayed silently for hundreds of people each week on my walks along Chicago streets. I would have given anything just to help one of them find God. No longer lonely, I yearned to help others find a way out of *their* loneliness. I wanted them to be able to walk in a dark world at the center of an unquenchable shaft of warm light. I wanted to help people with all my heart.

CHAPTER FOUR

A Victim of Grace

BY ERNEST GORDON

I cannot say when I found Christ," says Ernest Gordon, former dean of the chapel at Princeton University. "For one thing," he continues, "I am not sure that I ever lost Him. For another, I cannot say honestly that I ever went out of my way to look for Him. That He had found me is the truth of the matter! He did it before I was aware that He had. How long He had knocked on the door I do not know. It could have been since the moment when I was born!"

Gordon, the author of *Through the Valley of the Kwai,* elaborates:

I rather liked the thought of someone who was kindly and gentle, but I never understood where I might find Him. Oh yes, the Bible, some might say. But where in the Bible? John 3:16 perhaps. But I cannot remember learning the words. Yet I could always recite them. They conveyed that picture I had of Jesus as kindly and gentle. There was a ring of truth to them. If anything could cause me to raise my hat in reverence they did.

34

The words of John 3:16, however, were only a few beautiful ones in the midst of a mass of competing and cacophonous ones. I could associate them with home and with the serenity of church services—the simple, metrical psalms with their haunting melodies, the reverence expressed in the reading of the Bible lessons, the smell of damp walls, old Bibles, and well-scrubbed worshippers, the solemnity of bowed heads, the sense of another dimension.

The evidences of World War I were all around me. The top of our piano was lined with the photographs of uncles and second cousins who would never age. The camera had frozen them in the moment of their bright youth before pain creased their faces and death dulled their eyes.

The Depression, with its gray, chilling breath, came early for my family. My father was kept on in the army for about two years after the Armistice because he was a specialist, and he returned to a lesser position than the one he had held before the war, and to a loss of seniority. Unemployment without compensating benefits was the reward for his services. His silver and bronze medals were of little value, and we would have starved if my grandfather had not assigned to him his share of the inheritance that would have come to him.

As the shadows of the Depression darkened, so did the shadows of war. The smell of it was in the air. The message that I got early was that I was born in war to die in war. No sooner was I out of high school than I saw a notice in the Student Union of the University stating the need for young men to be trained as pilots in the Royal Air Force. The drums of war were beating and someone had to respond. I did. Not with enthusiasm but with a grim sense of duty.

A flaw in the metal of the plane I was flying caused a crash with the results that I enjoyed a respite in which to continue my studies, graduating just in time for World War II.

Because of injuries, I transferred to the infantry. By the fall of 1939 I was in the frontline in France and after France I was posted to Malaya via North Africa.

Back at university the news of Jesus had been dimmed, first of all by Christian groups who did not appear to have much to say about Him, and secondly by my own success in the discipline of Philosophy. It was an enjoyable mental game, but one that was far removed from the world confronting me.

However, the exigencies of battle (long forced marches in the night, dawn engagements, hunger, thirst, wounds, exhaustion, and fear) soon caused me to become a military stoic. The principle I developed was: If the worst can happen, it will—not only will it happen but it will be much worse than one can ever imagine. Events demonstrated the validity of this premise in a way that rationalism or romanticism could never have done. War is hell—the ultimate indignity, and prison camp is the lowest level of it: "the tenth circle."

After the fall of Singapore, I escaped to Sumatra on a naval patrol boat—my last command. On the way I picked up the survivors of a ship of the Royal Navy that had been destroyed by enemy action. Tom Rigden was its captain. Together we operated an escape route through which over a thousand escapees passed. Then we parted. I left in a thirty-five foot native sailing boat, with nine others, on the day the Japanese completed their bloodless conquest of Sumatra. Tom stayed behind to help administer the British forces in Padang.

But just two months later, almost out of the fighting, I was captured by a ship of the Grand Imperial Japanese Fleet. Four or five days later I was back in Singapore, and within a month I was packed off to Thailand with one of the first work parties to begin slaving on the Railway of Death in the Valley of the Kwai. Ultimately my destiny, after two-and-a-half years of toil and suffering, was the "death house" in the death camp, face-to-face with the last enemy.

It truly would have been so easy to die. I was paralyzed. I could take little nourishment. I had acute amoebic dysentery. And there was little food to take—less than two ounces of rice a day.

I heard the doctors say, "A couple of days at the most." But I said, in the words of Eliza Doolittle, "Not bloody likely." Death held all the aces, yet I did get out of the death house. Or rather I was carried out. Carried out by two good men who wanted me to die in peace. Carried out really because Tom Rigden had come into the death house to look for me.

When Tom reached the death camp, he asked, "Does anyone know Ernest Gordon?" Someone did.

"Where is he?" asked Tom.

"In the death house!"

"What's he doing there?"

"Dying, of course!"

So Tom came in to look for me. He walked down the long aisle with men on either side lying like sardines in a can. He passed right by me once, and no wonder. There was not much of me to see. I was thin

37

enough to put my two hands around my waist, and my face was concealed behind a beard. I tried to call his name but my voice was so weak that he did not hear me. Fortunately he came round a second time and by wagging an elbow like a bird with a broken wing, I caught his attention. He stopped and stared. "Good God, it isn't Ernest," he remarked. But I nodded to indicate that indeed it was.

Thus I got carried to a tiny little shack, six by six by six. At last I had the luxury of privacy—relatively speaking—and the absence of bedbugs and lice. I was out of the horror of that "tenth circle."

Shortly a Dr. MacIntosh popped his head through the tiny doorway to say, "Got good news for you. I've just received a supply of the medication you need. Enough to give you twelve injections. That should get rid of your dysentery." He filled a syringe from a glass capsule and stuck the needle into my arm. "There that's the first step."

It was only in 1961 that a friend wrote from Kuala Lumpur to say that by giving his gold watch to a Japanese guard to sell on the black market Tom Rigden had realized enough money to purchase that gift of medication. My friend truly wrote, "That was next door to giving up his own life for your sake, surely an echo of Jesus' words, 'Greater love hath no man than this, that he lay down his life for a friend.'"

That text (from John's Gospel) became the word of God in our midst. It was the message lived out by an increasing number of men in the camp and this message could not be ignored. It was "the saving word." Because of the dedicated nursing of two other friends, I was given the *second* step back to life. They not only nursed me but provided the extra nourishment I needed.

The pain of life was throbbing in my legs when a group of Australians visited me. They had a request: "We'd like you to come and teach us Christianity."

"Why me?" I asked.

"We've heard about you. Your blokes think you're all right, *and you've been at university*. You must know something!"

"But why do you want to study Christianity? I don't know I have a thing to teach you. Perhaps just the reverse."

"It's worth a try," was the reply. "There has to be *something* better than our current dog-eat-dog kind of existence. Maybe the better way is what Christianity is all about."

The sincerity of the appeal moved me to respond affirmatively, but I still didn't know exactly what I would teach. Then one of my nurses, "Dusty" Miller, came in with a basin of hot water and a rag with which to dress my ulcerated legs. "Here," he said, "you've been left this Bible." At this he handed me one of the books which the Bible Society had been distributing to soldiers. This one had been cared for and was covered with a piece of oilskin. The physical value was considerable—especially since paper from Bibles was regarded as best for rolling cigarettes! Why had one of my company highlanders willed the Bible to *me*?

Thus I, who barely knew the Christian faith at this point, began to teach it with the unexpected help of the Bible, and in the fellowship of these concerned men I learned with them that *the Gospels told the story of the better way for which we were all searching.* The Sermon on the Mount alone proclaimed it. The life and death of Jesus revealed it. We came to know Him as the man *we* ought to be. We also came to know Him as Emmanuel, *God with us.* Like the Apostles, we first knew Him as a man. Then came the time when we heard the question, "And who do *you* say that I am?" Before long we were able to answer, "Thou art the Christ, the Son of the Living God."

The Jesus I had dimly glimpsed in my childhood became the one I now saw to be "the only begotten Son of the Father, full of grace and truth." My life was no longer centered in myself, my country, my regiment, my philosophical system. It became centered in Him. And this experience was shared by at least 90 percent of the camp. *We were grasped by the living Christ.* We cared for each other. We saw Christ suffering with those who suffered and present at the dying of our comrades. In our prison camp, Jesus was giving us freedom—freedom in the spirit. In our death camp, He was giving us life—*eternal* life.

Thus our chaotic group of enslaved, nihilistic individuals became a community of life in which miracles happened. Not the kind of miracles some people wish for with bread dropping from heaven, neatly wrapped in plastic, nor freedom by which individuals were pulled out of an intolerable situation, but miracles of faith and love—the kind that happen when the impossible becomes possible. Out of nothing we created anesthetics, drugs, artificial limbs, Christmas plum puddings, a university, a symphony orchestra, and above all the miracle of forgiving our enemies. It had, of course, all happened before and is happening wherever and whenever people dare to bet their lives that Jesus Christ is Lord.

I was also called to preach. I preached regularly to *a minimum of three thousand* out of a camp of about four thousand. And what did I preach? The story of Jesus—His life, His teachings, His death, His resurrection, His ascension, His presence with us. I preached at least eight times on the parable of the Prodigal Son, and I did not exhaust it. It was a heady experience. I've known nothing like it since. Three-thousand-plus young men listening—not to me but to the word of the Living God who had found me! Listening so well that they were nourished by it and hungry for more.

In summing up, I can only say that the Word who comes to us in the mystery of "the word made flesh" is the Word of Freedom and Truth and Life. He is the Living Word who initiates the divine dialogue by which we are invited to respond as children to our Abba, our divine Father. And His first word is always one of welcome: "Come unto me all ye that labor and are heavy laden, and I will give you rest."

He is the Living Word who identifies Himself with us as flesh of our flesh and bone of our bone, and yet He is God. Thus we are given our identity. We know who we are because we know *whose* we are: we are Christ's and Christ is God's.

During my twenty-six years of campus ministry I knew many students who left the university in order to find themselves, and it was always my privilege to remind them that the only way they could accomplish this was through *repentance*. Only

by turning from ourselves and from all that impris-
ons us to Christ are we free to become the children of
God. Like the Prodigal we deserve only servitude, but
we are exalted by our divine Father's love to the
heights of sonship.

In the camp, Jesus was seen as the Living Word,
interpreting our human condition not in despair but
in hope. Our experience was that the grace of our
Lord Jesus surrounded us. I was aware of it in the lives
of those who were moved by the Holy Spirit to love
their comrades to the extent of risking, or giving,
their lives for them. But I would never have
understood "the height, depth, and breadth" of this
love if I had not studied the Scriptures and myself
learned to know "the only begotten of the Father, full
of grace and truth." And I think this quality of
understanding is part of the Pentecost experience. It
was in the understanding and teaching of the New
Testament that I experienced my own Pentecost
along with my brothers in Christ.

The power of sin is always that of separation,
division, alienation, and death. The power of God
in Christ, however, is the power of holiness, of
wholeness, of integrity, of fellowship, and of life. I
think that the Apostle Paul was saying something
like that when he wrote to the Colossians to tell
them that all things hang together in Christ. My
comrades and I were aware that it was the integrating
power of Christ that brought us together in such a
unity of fellowship that we prayed together, studied
together, and praised God together. The eternal life
we shared was the one in which we experienced our
unity in and with Jesus—who is what He said He
was: "I am the resurrection and the life. He that

believeth in me though he were dead yet shall he live, and whosoever believeth in me shall never die."

Thus I may only classify myself as *a victim of grace*, for my life in Christ is all grace—all given—not of my own deserving, but of the will, purpose, and love of the Eternal and Living God who has chosen to reveal Himself. Prison camps are built to keep prisoners in, but they can never be built strong enough to keep God out. In the freedom given by the act of Creation we choose to build prisons. By the act of Redemption, God in Christ has come, and comes, into these prisons to set us free.

CHAPTER FIVE

Sand in the Gears

JACK ROWLES

As I remember it, Jack Rowles appeared as one of the happy byproducts of the prayer and fellowship meetings that Ralston Young, a porter known as Red Cap 42, was holding on Track 13 in the Grand Central Station in New York City. These meetings were a spin-off of a weekly businessmen's meeting that met every Monday at Calvary House at 5:30 P.M. and that Ralston Young, the porter, attended once or twice a month. When this group was highlighted in a February 1946 article in the "Most Unforgettable Character" series in *Reader's Digest*, the curiosity of hundreds of New Yorkers was aroused. In the week after the article appeared, a succession of visitors came to the station, hoping to meet Ralston Young. Jack was one of the lucky ones for he appeared one noontime at the very hour when a group was actually in session, and somehow he found his way down into the dark railroad car on Track 13 while things were still humming. Ralston not only talked with Jack after the meeting but like an effective basketball player tossing the ball to a teammate, he highly recommended that Jack come to the Monday men's meeting at 61 Gramercy Park.

Jack looked up the Calvary House meeting the following week, which as a member of Sam Shoemaker's staff, I happened to be moderating. He possessed an unusually smooth exterior, having gone to school and college in the East and acquired—for good or ill—an unmistakable Ivy League manner. While the average newcomer at our Monday meetings usually showed some hesitancy in joining the circle of early arrivals, Jack felt no such timidity and, after the meeting came to order, was among the first visitors to introduce himself. He was a journalist, he said, a commuter with a house in White Plains and an office on West 46th Street, and was currently engaged in the specialized task of producing scripts for radio broadcasts. A member of a suburban church, he, like many businessmen, was failing to receive much benefit from his once-a-week religious activity on Sundays and was genuinely interested in hearing how other men were finding ways to use faith in their business work.

The talk that Monday was channelled into a discussion of honesty in business, kicked off by a salesman with a problem. This man's field was rubber goods and his difficulty arose from the fact that the was being asked to represent the products he was selling as having a superior quality which he believed they did not possess. "My job depends upon sales," he explained, "and sales occur when customers are persuaded that they can buy from me articles which are better than those available from my competitors. It's as simple as that. I can sell *if I lie* about my merchandise, but when this happens I end up quite 'out of conceit with myself.' You see I need help."

Fortunately there were three other men present that day who were facing the same or similar problems. One of these had found an answer by deciding to sell only on the basis of being absolutely honest about his goods in every situation, and while he admitted that he had lost a few sales, the net worth of his commissions had strangely enough not suffered. In fact, his business had increased. And something else had resulted from his recent experiences: his company, instead of criticizing his new sales policy, had taken a favorable view of it to the extent that they had begun to change the tenor of their promotional literature, making the copy truer and more accurate.

The rubber salesman laughingly refused to be completely convinced, but he admitted that he was impressed and had certainly been given something to think about. As for Jack Rowles, he was obviously fascinated and afterwards remembered that he had been especially grateful for a new definition of the word *sin*, which had been given during the course of the discussion. Someone had said that he had come to see that sin need not be an overt immoral or criminal act but rather was better defined as "any barrier standing between oneself and God" or, equally destructive, "between oneself and another person." This, said Jack, gave him a new handle to take hold of. It might explain some of the difficulties in his own home and also the over-competitiveness in his office. "If one looks at it this way, sin is very much like dirt in a piece of machinery."

He was running off to catch a train, so I asked him about lunch. Yes, he'd love to meet me some day and so we made a date.

A short time later we met at the old Princeton Club, which was not far from his office and also close to the station. He came armed with a carefully typed sheet of paper that he handed to me at the table. "Read this," he said. "It's what the A.A.s call a 'fearless moral inventory.' "

I opened it up. At the top was typed in caps: SAND IN THE GEARS. Under this heading came a list of specifics, which ran all the way from lack of interest in his children at home to the manner in which he had been handling his office expense account.

"Whew!" I gasped. "You've really covered the waterfront."

"Tried to. But take your time. That's my unsavory record. I haven't the slightest idea what to do about it."

As we continued to eat, I read over the paper more carefully, item by item. So many of the listings had parallels in events or habits in my own life.

"Reminds me of myself," I said grinning.

"Right. Glad to hear it. Now just what would you do about such a collection? It's one thing to see what's wrong but something else again to be free of the whole mess and started on a new chapter. What's the next step?"

I thought for a few minutes. Then, "If we were at 61 Gramercy Park," I said, "I'd suggest that we go straight into the church, kneel down in a convenient pew, and pray. But since we're a good twenty city blocks away, what do you say to walking over to the station and using Track 13 for the same purpose?"

Jack thought this was a great idea. No meeting would be taking place on the track. We'd have the familiar gloom of the darkened railway coach all to ourselves. And it made a perfect chapel. We found the spot in the next to the last car which Red Cap 42 always used, and quietly took a seat just behind the one used by the noonday group. Then, after a few minutes, without any prompting from me, Jack bent forward, rested his forehead on the back of the next seat, and eloquently expressed the sorrow he felt at being guilty of so many foolish, self-indulgent acts. At the end he asked God to forgive him and then, apparently feeling newly free and unfettered, offered as joyous a prayer of praise and thanksgiving as I had heard in many a day.

It was easy for me to follow with my own brief expression of gratitude for Jack's honesty and for the divine forgiveness which we both realized was so freely available to us, in the name of Jesus Christ—just for the asking.

After that it was pleasant to sit still for a few moments and enjoy the quiet peace of our informal sanctuary.

From then onwards Jack became a power in the Monday meetings and doubtless to a lesser degree in the Red Cap's meetings at the station. He was vocal, he was sympathetic, he was extremely practical. While he was only able to join us at "61" on the average of once or twice a month, it was quite evident that he had begun to live a new life. He always had a suggestion or two to make in the course of the meeting—or news of some significant spiritual event which had taken place in his work. He also told stories from time to time about the surprising new relationships with his wife and children, or about the quality of his writing which he felt had improved immeasurably.

About a year later, Sam Shoemaker (rector of Calvary Episcopal Church in New York and one of the organizers of the Gramercy Park meetings) was asked to give an important broadcast on evangelism over one of our national broadcasting systems. Sam knew what stories he wanted to tell and how he wanted to introduce his subject, but he was doubtful about the exact format of the broadcast and how to prepare the talk so that it would take the exact period of fourteen minutes. He had met Jack, and one morning the happy thought came to him that he should make use of Jack's special experience in putting the broadcast into final form. Jack was delighted to help. He greatly admired Sam and, though very busy with his own work, took over the broadcast and rewrote it completely. Not only this, but on the day of the broadcast he went along to Rockefeller Center in order to be present with Sam while he was speaking in the broadcasting booth.

This was a prize example of the kind of effective teamwork possible between a layman and a clergyman and so badly needed by the Protestant church in America if it is to take practical Christian faith out from the church sanctuary and into our nation. It also characterized the important help that Jack continued to give the work at Calvary as one of a number of valuable part-time volunteers.

CHAPTER SIX

Freedom from Fear

JAMES BELL NICOLL, M.D.

This is the story of an escape from fear so deep-rooted and strong that the answer an English medical man found through faith will perhaps help many others who suffer less acutely.

Before becoming a doctor, James Bell Nicoll served as a private in the British Expeditionary Force in Flanders in World War I. He was a mere boy at the time and underwent such a terrifying experience that he became ill and was sent to a military hospital for several months of nursing care. His body became strong again, but his mind never fully recovered. On returning home he found his whole life altered. He was especially afraid of being left alone. Any spot a quarter to a half-mile removed from other people created in him a childish, unreasoning, blind panic. The psychologists called it *agoraphobia*, fear of open or public spaces, a condition often cured by uncovering the source of the disturbance. But despite visiting more than one foremost English psychologist, the ex-soldier was not helped in the slightest.

As the years went by, he came to accept irrational fear as part of his make-up, an inevitable and incurable trait and something that must be hidden from everyone including his own family. In his difficulties he felt that he had only one cause for thankfulness—the mental condition did not affect him in his car, and therefore his work was unaffected. His practice in Surrey flourished.

One spring he was invited to attend a week of religious meetings at an Anglican retreat center, Lee Abbey, in North Devon. He was not especially interested in the church but he decided to accept the invitation, as Lee Abbey was pleasantly located on the sea and offered the prospect of a holiday in rather unusual and, he hoped, refreshing surroundings. He was not disappointed. As for the people he met, their earnestness and eagerness struck him at first rather unpleasantly but his amused tolerance turned into a measure of appreciation when he attended his first morning meeting. What he heard all seemed to be good, sound stuff, even though he thought himself one step removed from it.

On the second evening, however, he became much more interested. The chief speaker was a middle-aged clergyman, Jack Winslow, whom the staff referred to as their chaplain. In a very personal way, he spoke at some length on prayer. His experience he said convinced him that individuals should set aside an unhurried period of an hour each morning for private devotions. Then he went on to present a five-fold prayer plan for beginners. He used the letters that make up the word *psalm* for this. "Let us think of P," said Jack, "as standing for *praise*; S for *self-surrender*; A for *asking*; L for *listening*; and M for *meditation*."

51

This plan impressed the doctor as an entirely new and very practical conception. Intrigued, he started reviewing his life, wondering just what would be involved in becoming a Christian himself. As he kept thinking further about this, on reaching his room, he realized that his major hesitation simply came from the fear that he might not be able to stay the course. He might make it for twenty-four hours, but he hesitated to start something with a bang only to have it fizzle out. However, he finally concluded that he should give the Christian experiment a whirl.

A most uncomfortable night followed. He woke up every hour or so, recalling some fresh sin which he supposed would have to be confessed and dealt with if he were to go ahead.

He arose early, dressed, and at 6:30 A.M. hied himself to the chapel with the intention of engaging in an hour of private prayer along the lines suggested by the previous night's talk. He started with P for *praise* and found that he could spontaneously thank God for His goodness and do so with a grateful heart. Then he passed on to *surrender*. But now he at once saw how far he was from any true attitude of obedience to the will of God in the details of his daily life. As he knelt there, he realized that he could no longer pray, that he would have to make a deliberate choice to see God's plan for himself or abandon the experiment entirely. Then in the quiet of that sanctuary he found himself saying, "Lord, I surrender my life entirely into thy keeping. Take me and show me whatever I may be keeping back, and help me to give up those things too."

At this point a clergyman entered the chapel and began to prepare to celebrate Holy Communion.

Others followed him. The doctor decided to stay, and by participating in the service received an unexpected blessing for which, without being able to express it in words, he also felt extremely grateful.

Lee Abbey is situated in the Lorna Doone country of North Devon. The property runs along high cliffs overlooking the sea and includes a promontory known as Jennifer's Leap, an eerie spot from which a forlorn maiden is reputed to have cast herself to death on the rocks far below. When the doctor had made his way outside, he unconsciously took a path through the woods leading to this spot. After not more than a hundred yards he realized where he was, and quite clearly a voice seemed to be saying to him, "Go on to Jennifer's Leap." Only the day before no amount of money could have tempted him to proceed, but now he continued to walk ahead. He suddenly felt very much alone, and the old panic began to return—clammy hands, rapidly beating heart, quick breathing, all the trappings. But now he prayed, asking God to deliver him from this fear, and in a second or two the fear simply vanished. It seemed like shedding an uncomfortable garment. He could hardly grasp what had happened. He was free, a free man after twenty-nine years. He was so excited that he ran forward right to the edge of the cliff and, as he stood there, had not a qualm.

A number of thoughts had come to mind as he began his walk. One was that for him cigarettes should be out. For most of mankind he supposed that commitment of one's life to God would not necessarily involve such an act, but for him it seemed essential.

There followed a day of special inner peace and refreshment, but at dawn the next morning he rose and made his way directly to the same lonely spot on the cliff in order to test the reality of his experience. To his joy he had not a trace of panic. Actually the fear never returned, and he was convinced that it never would. Walking alone became one of his greatest pleasures, and he found that the lonelier he was, the more real the presence of God would often become.

His medical profession took on a fresh dimension and as time went on, he was overjoyed at seeing that his newfound faith proved a very special help to an increasing number of patients.

The story of one of these patients sums up dramatically the extent of the doctor's new influence. A woman who lived some forty miles away had reached the end of the line and was planning to commit suicide. She had decided on the practical step of stuffing paper into the chinks of her kitchen windows and then turning the gas stove on full blast, unlighted.

She happened to start by tearing up the copy of a magazine in which the doctor's spiritual experience had been printed. The heading, "The Fear Vanished," caught her eye, and she stopped to read the article. It made her realize that fear of the future and of a divided family was at the heart of her depression, and as she read along she found that in some strange way the pressure had lessened. Someone else, not forty miles away, had solved this problem, someone with an M.D. after his name. His address was given. She reached for a bit of writing paper and briefly wrote a note, asking if the doctor and she might meet. Then she determined to hold off any drastic action and wait for results.

In due course the doctor received the moving little note and at once, feeling sure that he could help, talked to the woman on the telephone, and arranged to meet her within a day or two in a town about halfway between their two homes. The woman simply needed to hear the account of what had happened to him at Lee Abbey. Sitting in one of the cars, they talked for two hours or more. Two points became clear: (1) the relative unimportance of many of life's unpleasant experiences, and (2) the availability of the supernatural action of God's own love and forgiveness.

There was no more thought of suicide, and at the next harvest festival the doctor was surprised by the gift of a turkey from his grateful friend and patient.

CHAPTER SEVEN

The Turning Point

KAY LIMBURG

There was one Jewish family at the hotel in Vermont that summer, a very attractive couple with two young children, a boy and a girl. The husband, Alan, held a seat on the New York Stock Exchange but was enjoying a long vacation. His wife, Kay, was outgoing and friendly and was obviously well-liked by the eighty or ninety other guests. They both played golf and tennis extremely well and entered whole-heartedly into all of the usual activities of the summer colony.

I remember meeting Kay first at one of the informal dances of which there were two or three a week. "Come," a friend said, "there's a new guest here whom I want you to know." With that he led me out on the dance floor and cut in on Kay, and thus began a warm friendship. My first impression was of a person very light on her feet and with an excellent sense of humor. I can't remember what started us laughing, but that first dance seemed delightful and we were able to circle the floor a couple of times before her husband interposed. I yielded reluctantly and with the sure intention of returning for another dance at the first opportunity—which came a bit later that same evening.

A couple of days after this we met accidentally on the hotel veranda, following breakfast. "I've been so surprised," she began, "to learn that you are a clergyman."

"Yes," I admitted. "Actually I do very little preaching, but I am an ordained minister and, except for this month of August, keep very busy in a number of ways on the staff of a church down on Gramercy Park, New York."

Then I realized that she wanted to talk.

"Alan and I have no real church here at all," she said. "Occasionally we go to the Friday night service at the big synagogue on Fifth Avenue, just across from the entrance to Central Park. But we live outside the city in White Plains, and most of the time we don't bother. I realize we're missing something."

"Well, perhaps you'd like to come down to one of our midweek meetings on 21st Street," I suggested. "Personally I'm very keen about these. They're somewhat unusual in that most of the evening is devoted to hearing businessmen and women and professional and family people talk about faith from their own experience—how they've found faith and what a difference it is making in their lives."

My new acquaintance immediately seemed keen to come. Her father, she explained, lived in New York City, and she and her husband often spent the night in town at his apartment. She had never heard of religious meetings at which ordinary people spoke about their personal faith, and she thought that both of them would like to come down some evening in the autumn and see what was happening.

We left it at that. But then other talks followed, more immediate in their implications. In the dining room, at the dances, wherever we happened to meet, the conversation inevitably turned to the subject of personal faith. Like many Americans, Kay believed strongly in the existence of a creator, but the question was how one was to think of Him. She instinctively craved a deeper understanding. Was there any special way, she asked rather skeptically, by which an individual might come to know Him personally? Yes, I assured her. In fact there were two very simple ways. One was through the life of Jesus Christ and the other through practicing personal prayer. "Fortunately," I explained, "at a certain time, in a certain place, there lived a Jew, Jesus of Nazareth, who in His life and teachings wonderfully revealed both the nature of God and the way individual men and women may live under the power and inspiration of His Spirit. The story is all down in black and white."

Then the very next time I saw her, she laughingly waved a book in the air. It turned out to be a Gideon Bible, which she had discovered in her cabin.

"You see I've lost no time in finding a Bible," she declared. "But it's a bit formidable. I'm not sure how to tackle it."

"Well, that's great. And you don't have to read it from cover to cover. Here let me have it for a minute." I opened it and turned to the New Testament and pointed out the books of Mark and Luke. "The heart of the matter is right there," I said. "The story in Mark gives the shortest account of Jesus' life; conceivably one could read this whole

58

Gospel, as it is called, at a sitting. But I don't recommend that. Instead, take it in small doses—perhaps a chapter at a time. Or begin reading until you come to a scene that particularly interests you or to a verse or two which you don't understand. Stop there and give it some thought. We can talk about the difficulties. You're sure to find some. It helps to know the background and constantly try to read between the lines."

And so she began. By rising a bit earlier, she found time every morning to read a further section of the story the book of Mark had to tell about Jesus. And it was her good fortune to feel that this study of His life was not so much a chore as an adventure. Sometimes at luncheon she came along with a comment, or a question, or what she considered an exciting discovery. Most of what she read was apparently quite fascinating. She had no difficulty in accepting accounts of the miracles; it was only some of Christ's teachings which troubled her. One of her first "puzzlements" centered on a verse that had once bothered me: "For he that hath, to him shall be given: and he that hath not, from him shall be taken even that which he hath" (4:25). "You know that sounds most unfair. How could Jesus have said anything like that?" she asked.

I could sympathize. "Yes, that's a tough one," I admitted. "But look at it this way: 'To have not' represents a negative attitude of mind if you dwell on it. When I grouse about my health or complain because other people seem to be better off than I, I'm really indulging in self-pity. And if I continue to complain, I become a downright bore. I drive people away from me—even my best friends. Thus I lose, almost automatically, one of the most valuable assets of my life, and as time goes on I become infinitely poorer. It's a rather basic principle in life, and you'll find that Jesus was always much more interested in principles than in mere rules and precepts. The counterpart is that a person who is grateful and recognizes his blessings wins friends and much besides."

She saw the point and was at least partially reassured. Thus her knowledge of the New Testament was steadily increasing. But not much was happening in the area of personal prayer. Quite the reverse. The more she tried to pray, she said, the more futile her efforts seemed. She even felt silly, waiting there in her cabin in the morning for something to happen and drawing "nothing but a blank." "I sit there alone, wishing to find reality in 'meditation'— trying, as you put it, to 'practice the presence of God' and simply become very self-conscious and even annoyed."

I didn't know how to help her. But God Himself was at work. One morning she suggested that I drive to town with her. Her husband had gone to New York, and she had a number of errands. It was a lovely, sunny day. The air was fresh and the surface of the lake sparkled. As we drove by one of the loveliest spots on the lake, I suggested that we stop for a few minutes. So we parked the car and crossed the flat rocks to a place from which we could see the full length of the lake. Sitting there, we saw all the beauty of Vermont in the panorama before us. I at least quietly felt a sense of God's presence.

Rather timidly I said, "Perhaps God would speak to you here."

Kay looked around in obvious alarm. The public road was close by, other people might be passing. To her the idea of praying in such a place apparently seemed frightening. I kept my mouth shut, however, but closed my eyes. I had no idea of what might happen next but at least I could overcome my own self-consciousness. Then my companion must have followed suit. At least neither of us spoke again for what seemed to be a considerable length of time. Finally, curiosity got the better of me, and I glanced up. Here was this woman with head lowered and her own eyes tightly shut. I thought, "I wonder if this is it?" I glanced out across the lake. Even the waves were still; I couldn't move. The experience was almost like a spell. Finally Kay came to. With an expression on her face more eloquent than any words could have been, she made it abundantly clear that the silence had not been wasted. Then she stood up and went back to the car.

We drove the rest of the way to town in comparative silence. It was only on the return trip that she said a word about the time on the rocks and then it was almost a casual reference. "I guess I got my answer," she said, leaving it to me to interpret the words as best I could. Even during the following days she never said very much about that morning. But there were a few passing references now and then: "Ever since that time on the rocks . . ." she might say—or words to that effect, implying that whatever had taken place that day by the lake shore had represented a kind of turning point in her spiritual experience. She had no more complaints about lack of reality in prayer, no more reference to uncertainty and frustration regarding her own devotional life.

Up to this point, as a Jew, Kay felt that she would be a traitor to accept Jesus fully as the Power of God's Holy Spirit. She felt she could accept God wholeheartedly but not Christ as His equal. She had surrendered her will to be open to God's will, but she could not think of herself as a Christian.

Then Alan and she unexpectedly had a bitter fight, one that made each feel that their marriage should be at an end. Both were very angry. At that point Kay unexpectedly experienced a fresh, mystical experience of Jesus. It seemed to her that He was stretching His arms out to her personally and saying, "If you will live up here with me, none of your earthly problems need to hurt you. It's only as you turn and take them on in your own strength that they pull you down."

Kay's reaction was to respond affirmatively to the invitation she felt a living Christ was offering her. She decided to accept Him as the Power of God and a much deeper change took place within her. The marriage was saved, and she found that the Holy Spirit was now bringing victory out of frustration.

That autumn Alan and Kay did appear at our Gramercy Park meetings at Calvary House. After one of these Alan drew me aside and thrust an envelope into my hands. "Here," he said, "here's a small gift. Put it into your expense account or use it in the work here at Calvary House. It's not much but I want to give it to you with thanks. Oh, don't ask me to explain. Let's just say it's a token of the relief I feel."

CHAPTER EIGHT

Four Steps to a New Life

BY IRVING HARRIS

Certain people find a new life suddenly, and their nature and outlook become different overnight. Others of us come into the Christian way more slowly or at least a step at a time.

It took at least four spiritual upheavals to turn me into the kind of person whom God could count on, and it was only after the last of these experiences that I found a quality of life that began to communicate faith effectively to other people.

The first of these experiences happened at Camp Dudley on Lake Champlain, the oldest organized camp for boys in the United States, when I was quite unexpectedly asked to take an older man's place and preach at a Sunday morning chapel service. I had been spending my summers at Dudley for a number of years, and as mentioned in my book *The Breeze of the Spirit*, I was both terrified and flattered by this chance. The moment I was asked to talk I knew what I wanted to try to say. Camp gave those of us who spent time there the vision of choosing a vocation that related to the welfare of other people. Such a vision differed greatly from the competitive spirit most of us were in the habit of expressing at school and college, and it seemed important to start the talk by mentioning it as a live and desirable option for one's life work, and then urging campers to make a decision on the strength of such a vision. I also realized that such a choice would undoubtedly involve self-denial, and this in turn would require determination and perseverance. Something about courage should certainly round out the talk.

Loading my portable typewriter, I started on such a talk—vision . . . decision . . . courage—and the words fairly flowed. When I finished, I decided I would learn my talk by heart, and I found a quiet place in the woods where I could go over the script and practice aloud. Then a funny thing happened. I realized that the sermon was already being delivered and that I was the congregation. I was preaching to myself. As Sunday approached, I became more and more uncomfortable. Dudley is a very large camp, and I realized that what I said would be viewed critically by dozens of my own best friends. And the talk might represent a challenge to many who heard it. As a matter of fact I felt challenged by it myself. When Saturday afternoon arrived I reached a kind of impasse: could I get up the following morning and give such a talk if I had not faced up to its challenge myself? It seemed to me that the Lord must have a sense of humor. You see, my own vision had already pointed to the Christian ministry, but this was a work I more than half dreaded and so had been postponing any decision about it. Now I felt backed into a corner—either I would have to agree to the ministry as my life's work or go to the camp director and tell him that I couldn't give the sermon. For a while it was touch and go. But when I finally said yes, a terrific burden seemed to fall off my back and a sense of joy welled up within me that completely dispelled the acute sense of fear I had had at the prospect of preaching. I was a free man, and when the time came I almost relished the chance to stand up and speak. Surely it must have been about the best talk I ever gave.

That weekend marched me straight out of Wall Street, where I had taken a conventional job on graduating from Princeton, and entirely altered my daily work. While I had previously been a member of a church, that first sermon undoubtedly formed the occasion of my actually becoming a Christian.

A second upheaval followed shortly. It so happened that I had signed a contract to undertake work at the Princeton University Press, and I felt obligated to invest at least a year in this job even though I would eventually be returning to the academic world.

I took up residence at The Nassau Club in Princeton and lived there continuously until I went to a theological school. Early that autumn Sam Shoemaker, a man I had been criticizing and running away from, got hold of me and suggested that I should reread the life of Christ in one of the new modern translations of the New Testament. I went about this secretly and reluctantly, for I was quite convinced that I already knew all about Jesus' life and His teaching. How wrong I was! I bought a James Moffatt translation of the New Testament and began with the Gospel of Mark. From the very start of my morning readings, the figure of a person emerged so magnetic in His personality and so perfect in His behavior that I became fascinated and challenged. The way He dealt with people and situations was so far superior to my own behavior that I took a yellow pad and for clarity's sake jotted down at the top a summary of Jesus' outstanding character traits. After a few days I then drew a line across the middle of the sheet, below which I began to list the un-Christian things showing up in my own life. In less than two weeks I had listed thirty-nine examples of acts and reactions in my behavior radically different from those in the Bible story. Many of my attitudes and acts caused me a deep sense of shame. Fortunately, at the same time, I recalled how central forgiveness was in Jesus' teaching and I realized that however undeserving I might be, I could count on God for another chance. In what seemed something of a mystery, I also saw that this chance was available because of Jesus' own faithfulness.

One morning I dropped to my knees by the bed, like a little child, admitting my sense of shame to God and telling Him I was truly sorry for the self-indulgences and waste in my way of living. And right then and there something inexplicable happened. I felt cleansed and I felt renewed—both at the same time. And the miracle was that at the very moment of my deepest regret, I could rejoice in the certainty that the past was *past* and the future could be different. The second chance I wanted was definitely being given to me. Afterwards, when I got circulating, everything around me seemed different— the men at the breakfast table, even the bacon and eggs.

The content of my religious comprehension had been vastly increased during those few days, and the deeper understanding and inner purification were so palpable that I had no hesitation in believing this experience to be a fresh conversion. At least it marked another turning point and gave meaning to what lay ahead.

Though a Presbyterian, I was welcomed for the next academic year at the Episcopal Theological Seminary in Alexandria, Virginia, and there I made a further discovery that immeasurably enriched my inner life. The classroom work interested and benefited me greatly, but it was an event quite separate from my new studies about which I want to write.

My roommate and I were accustomed to get up early and use the first half-hour of the day for personal devotions. One morning I was reading in the Gospel of Luke when the twelfth verse in the sixth chapter caught and held my attention: "And it came to pass . . . that [Jesus] went out into a mountain to pray, and continued all night in prayer to God." This was on the night before He chose the twelve disciples. What struck me here in particular were the two words *all night*. How inadequate these made my own prayer life seem—my ten or fifteen minutes in the morning and five or ten minutes at night! It was clear that I would have to shake myself and do better. One can't copy Jesus, but anyone trying to follow Him doubtless must learn how to meditate and wait upon God. To try to pray all night would be ridiculous, but I could start to experiment with shorter periods of silence. What, I asked myself, would it be like to pray, say, for an hour?

I happened to have free time regularly after lunch. That afternoon instead of returning to my room, where interruptions would be inevitable, or to the library, I took one of the country roads leading away from the school. After a short walk, and feeling rather foolish, I ducked under a barbed-wire fence, crossed a pasture, and stopped under the branches of a huge oak. What happened next I later called "two-way prayer." With closed eyes I stood quietly, neither offering up petitions nor asking God directly for anything. I felt relaxed and very much at peace, and I had a rather vivid sense of God's presence. After what seemed like a long period of silence, I glanced at my wristwatch. About twelve minutes had passed! However, while surprised, I wasn't discouraged. In fact, I stayed alone for the full hour and then, day by day, for the next week or so, I returned eagerly to the same pasture and tree.

By the end of a week I found myself raising up questions before God to which I needed answers—practical ones, especially one or two having to do with study plans for the next year when I would be leaving Virginia. And it was encouraging to sense a response. God did speak to me—in the sense that He gave me deep, inner convictions of the rightness and wrongness of the different lines of action I might take, and He put into my mind thoughts which I know I would not have entertained had it not been for the silence I was keeping. Thus a most unexpected solution came to a query about my next seminary work, an original and rather difficult plan of procedure—one I would never have conceived of on my own.

This inner light, clear and completely convincing, represented a new dimension in my comprehension and the practice of the religious life. A new chapter opened.

Perhaps the most significant episode of the four upheavals then took place in Oxford, England, where I went sightseeing after a strenuous winter as a student at New College, Edinburgh. The theology and church history that I studied in Scotland had been fascinating, but I felt ready for a change, and after visiting a number of English cathedrals (like hundreds of Americans before me), I arrived at Oxford, intending to inspect several of the ancient colleges and then fly to France for a few days in Paris.

News had reached me that a Princeton classmate and his wife had taken up residence in Oxford for the spring term, and this gave me an added incentive to go there rather than to Cambridge. After locating an inexpensive room, I found my friends' whereabouts and paid them a call, expecting to pick up the latest news from home. They had an attractive flat near one of the colleges, and to my surprise at the time I called, their living room was fairly bursting with visitors. Among these I met an unusually handsome Scotsman, an undergraduate at Christ Church College, who, like me, had been in World War I.

As we talked, he launched into an enthusiastic description of a student gathering planned for a small hotel about eight miles down the river and set to begin the very next day. He warmly urged me to attend. For several reasons I had a holy horror of becoming involved in such an event, and I at once, and none too graciously, declined the Scotsman's invitation on the grounds that I wanted to devote my time to seeing the university.

The Oxonian looked at me rather caustically, sensing my overly reserved attitude and smiled.

"Don't you think it's rather childish," he said, "to be negative about something about which you have no firsthand information?"

Reluctantly I smiled back and agreed. Whereupon it was decided that we would leave the final decision open so that, if I had a change of heart, I would join the party the next day at a local rendezvous, the famous Mitre Hotel.

What a difference a simple choice sometimes makes in one's destiny! That next day proved another turning point. Somewhat sheepishly I appeared at the hotel and, within an hour, found myself at a charming inn in the village of Wallingford. Twenty or more other students had already arrived and they appeared an extremely attractive group. After meeting a number of them I had a chance to stretch my legs on a pleasant country stroll with a medical student from South Africa, a Rhodes Scholar.

The meetings, which began after supper, were very informal, the group sitting in a circle and being led by one of their own number as a moderator. There were short introductions, answers to questions, and considerable laughter. I felt very much at home and surprisingly interested as the question was raised as to what influence college students might have in our turbulent, chaotic world. From the start I realized that I would have missed a special, personal benefit had I not come.

My Scottish acquaintance himself took the session on Saturday morning. He spoke unhurriedly about a recent spiritual experience, which he described as altering his whole perspective on life. He went into detail both about his war experiences and his current college life; in fact he compared them. In France where he had served for almost two years as a captain in a Highland regiment, he claimed that the physical danger and rough life in the trenches had caused him much less mental distress than the inner conflicts he had more recently suffered in adjusting to life at Oxford. In France his position had been clearly recognized and firmly fixed. At Oxford, by contrast, his relationships were extremely fluid, and he had secretly been jockeying for position within the framework of the undergraduate world, constantly wondering what his collegemates were really thinking about him. Even the choice of a necktie and other wearing apparel became a matter of top importance. Popularity, or being accepted as "one of the boys," took precedence over everything else and he found himself harassed by doubts and plagued with inner distress that often seemed unbearable. Then he said that by "accepting the lordship of Jesus Christ" he had found an unexpected release. Through the wisdom of a small band of Christians, he woke up to the truth that actually he need compare himself with no one else—that as long as he was aiming to act in ways pleasing to God, he had "nothing to prove" and "nothing to defend."

While the speaker was describing his old hang-ups, I felt an uncanny sense that he was describing to a tee my own limitations. As he concluded, I'm quite sure I uttered an audible sigh and when the meeting broke up I strongly wished to talk with him. This man obviously had found a kind of personal freedom that I still lacked but deeply desired. I sidled around the edge of the group and grabbed the speaker's arm.

"Look," I began, "if a fellow can reach the point where he doesn't care what other people think of him, that must be heaven on earth. How do you go about it?" The Scotsman faced me and laughed.

"Basically," he said, "it's a question of handing over to God the control of one's life. Quite simple but rather costly."

"Well, I'm trying my best to serve Him," I protested.

"Yes, I know. You are learning a lot about God and doing many things for Him. But you are still managing your life yourself. What I'm talking about takes a deliberate act of dedication in which you say in so many words, 'Here, Lord, here's my life—lock, stock, and barrel—from this point on out. It's yours to take and use in any way you yourself wish. You are now the owner.' Have you ever said that?"

I had to admit I never had.

"Well, there's no time like the present."

I reacted negatively. "You don't mean right here and now, in a crowded room like this with people all around."

"Certainly," he answered. "There's a corner right here. We can have it all to ourselves. Let's have a spot of prayer. You tell the Lord that you want Him to take over more fully, and then I'll pray for you."

Actually nothing could have been simpler. We were sitting close together. Without changing my position, I simply bowed my head, and the words poured out as if such an occasion had been long overdue. "I've been hanging on to myself," I admitted, "I've been my own boss, and now I'd like to give the whole works back to you, Father." That was the gist of what I said, and the feeling of rightness and release that followed was both unexpected and indescribable.

Then my mentor prayed, heartily and briefly, after which we stood up and, with a happy sense of accomplishment and spiritual liberty, shook hands.

At an evening meeting I found the chance to make a progress report. It was well received.

We returned to Oxford in high fettle and I with a firm intention to review all my plans for the future. As I took counsel with a few of my new companions, I set a new course and changed my priorities. In Scotland the role of the preacher had stood out preeminently as very important. I now saw that a number of other activities would have to come first and there would have to be a better balance between study and *time with people*. I also saw a dozen reasons for spending the spring in England rather than back in the more formal atmosphere of a Scottish university.

The authorities in Edinburgh gladly agreed to my withdrawal from a third term of classroom work there, without jeopardizing the completion of my theological courses and ordination.

Two other matters of special importance were also soon dealt with. Instead of continuing on to France for a further holiday I freely offered the little nest egg I had reserved for this to one of my Oxford friends who obviously needed help with his personal expenses.

The third question was a highly personal one involving a shady act that I had committed as an undergraduate back at Princeton. It was something I had completely forgotten until I began to find fellowship with those at Oxford. It had been buried in some subconscious area of my mind. But my new friends—who, by the way, called themselves "A First Century Christian Fellowship"—had adopted specific principles to test their behavior. These were based on a summary of Jesus' Sermon on the Mount, which had been prepared by an outstanding American lay Christian, Robert E. Speer. They centered on the virtues of honesty, purity, unselfishness, and love. As a goal for Christian behavior Dr. Speer had put the word *absolute* in front of each, making a high, four-fold code for followers of Jesus Christ to aim at. I was brought up short one day by that very first principle, absolute honesty. I was shocked to recall the misuse of funds while chairman of a college dance committee. It had been my job to raise and dispense comparatively large sums of money in the course of arranging three large "proms," and to my acute discomfiture I now remembered that, while my accounting for the most part had been extremely accurate, after the last dance I had definitely cheated. Some of the profits on this occasion had found their way into my private purse to be spent secretly on the purchase of an expensive winter overcoat. Though chairmen of dance committees had formerly been allowed to profit personally if their social projects ended in the black, this had *not* still been the case at the time I had inherited the responsibility. In the light of my new awareness of God's truth I had to admit that what I had done was nothing less than stealing. And it was a goodly amount, over four hundred dollars. When I took an opportunity to talk over this college mischief with one of my Oxford friends, he helped me to see how I could report the matter to Princeton authorities and arrange to restore the amount of money I had taken.

That spring it was my good luck to be in on the beginning of what, through the newspapers in South Africa, was soon called "The Oxford Group." After Wallingford the work spread quickly. I watched it grow and, in a small measure, participated in it. As meetings took place, first in my friends' apartment and then in a number of colleges, I was occasionally asked to speak. On the first occasion I came very near flopping. An American at Balliol College gathered a good-sized group of undergraduates together in his room one Sunday afternoon and after establishing order asked me to lead off. Caught unaware I was simply tongue-tied and could think of not a single sensible remark. "Nothing to prove." Yes, I had nothing to prove and nothing to say, until our host most happily suggested that I recount what had happened to me at the weekend down the river. That was simple enough. And "nothing is so persuasive in religion as just the story of a personal experience." I got going and there was a real response.

To be honest I must admit that, during my further residence in Oxford, I awoke nearly every morning with a somewhat chilling sensation and a vague realization that I had taken a step into the unknown. For better or for worse I had abandoned my customary fixed schedule and had also become an intimate part of an active spiritual family or team. Since these new intimates began their day with Bible study and "listening prayer," I too launched out on a more regular and less hurried period of morning devotions in which, as instructed, I sought definite knowledge of the will of God and, as "guidance" from the Holy Spirit, detailed directions on the use of my time. The results were rather exciting, however they might be explained.

For instance, the name of one student who lived just across the road kept flashing into my mind. I had met him at the Balliol College meeting, and the thought kept coming in my "quiet time" that possibly he was someone for whom I had a special word of counsel. Rather conceited this seemed but not to be ignored. After all, I thought, no undergraduate can resent an invitation for tea or a walk.

After a bite of food I accordingly, if somewhat reluctantly, strolled over to this fellow's college, entered the main quad, and yelled up at an open window which the porter pointed out as the student's room. A head appeared and in answer to my invitation to tea a voice replied, "Yes, I would like that, but what are you doing right now?" My plans were entirely flexible and the result was that the undergraduate, a South African, and I had a delightful hour walking across the adjacent meadows. More important, a story I told him about a miserable year I had once had at Harvard Law School proved of personal value since my companion was unhappily wrestling with a number of pre-med courses for which he felt wholly unqualified and had been wanting the courage to write his family and ask them if he could switch to another study major.

That same week I received a note from two roommates at University College, who also had been at the Balliol meeting, inviting me to breakfast. Here again the occasion produced spiritual results: these two students became involved in the enlarging fellowship, and I began to see better what might be called the claims of Christ on the rising generation of university students.

And so it went, with almost every day bringing some further "guided event"—a chance to speak about faith, a new group of inquirers, even a university service at which the chaplain referred to the signs of revival evident on so many sides.

In all, I had nine weeks at Oxford, at the end of which I felt compelled to return to Edinburgh as a messenger of good news. There, a roomful of fellow seminarians welcomed me in a private residence, and I was encouraged to make a full report of what I had experienced and seen happening in the South. The excursion to Scotland, before I sailed home from Liverpool, resembled a whirlwind, but I came away humbly grateful and ready to make personal evangelism the main emphasis of my life.

CHAPTER NINE

Into and Out of a Million Dollars

MILLARD FULLER

Few people succeed in amassing a fortune only to give it away. But Millard Fuller* did just that. Let me tell you his story—and that of his wife Linda.

The background is something like this. Millard grew up in a small town in Alabama where his father bought him a pig with instructions to fatten him up, sell him, and make himself some money. He did just that and enormously enjoyed the experience of being a successful businessman. More pigs followed, plus chickens and rabbits and, when his dad bought a farm, he changed to the cattle business. This paid his way through college and by the time he reached law school at the University of Alabama he and a friend had branched out into various kinds of money-making enterprises and were raking in at least thirty thousand dollars a year.

One of his lines was selling advertising for large desk blotters for students. He started pounding the

*Millard Fuller can be written to at Habitat for Humanity, Inc., 419 West Church Street, Americus, Georgia 31709.

pavement in a number of college towns where there were motion picture theaters. At a theater in Tuscaloosa, Alabama, he asked to see the manager about purchasing ad space on a desk blotter. While waiting for him, he got chatting with a girl at the ticket window. My, but she was attractive! As things turned out he did not get an ad and found that the girl had gone home before he emerged again in the lobby. Millard had an idea that the girl's last name was Caldwell, and he made up his mind to return to his college room and call up every Caldwell in town. He got several answers. One young lady seemed especially pleasant and as they continued chatting, they found they enjoyed talking to each other.

All at once the girl said, "By the way, how tall are you?"

Millard answered, "Six-feet-four."

"Really," said the young lady. "I'm five-feet-ten." And right then Millard knew he'd found his date for the evening!

He and Linda had a long talk in the local student cafeteria. A year later, in August 1959, they were married.

The week before the wedding they drew up a covenant, pledging to "outlove each other . . . not to have secrets *and* to seek and maintain a right relationship with God." It was a solemn compact, and they had it framed to hang over their bed.

One would say, so far so good, but actually the marriage proved quite incidental to Millard's business affairs, which were constantly marching forward at a rapid pace. For several reasons he and his law partner, Morris Dees, had established themselves in Montgomery, the capital of the state, and

Fuller and Dees, Inc., a mail-order and publishing business, soon occupied substantial office space near the center of town. Linda was one of an increasing number of clerks or secretaries, and so was by no means idle herself, but to her the growth of the business was all rather confusing, and she was seeing less and less of a husband whose activities were keeping him more and more away from home—even after the birth of two children.

With Millard's sharp mind and uncanny ability to make more money than the average chap his age, Fuller and Dees boomed. It had been selling everything from cookbooks (they became the largest cookbook publisher in the nation) to refurbished apartment houses. One item alone, comfortable cushions for farm tractors, made a net profit of seventy thousand dollars in three months.

One morning the treasurer of the company walked into Millard's office and announced that Millard had become a millionaire! Millard thought this over for a few minutes and then said, "O.K. Let's now shoot for *ten million*."

In his case the sudden financial success exacted a heavy toll. The farther up the financial ladder Millard climbed, the greater number of troubles he found facing him—and these were by no means just business headaches. In one of his books he lists these headaches specifically:

(1) His most valued link with the Church broke apart.

(2) A chance to visit Africa and survey conditions in a number of mission fields, which he would have loved to do, miscarried.

(3) The desire for wealth displaced every other

goal and any activity to help extend the Kingdom of God was postponed to a later date. "Oh, well," he reasoned, "I'll probably do such work later. It's not a convenient time now."

Unconsciously Millard also became exceedingly dishonest. And even his health began to break down. Under his mounting business pressure, he suddenly found himself with serious breathing problems, literally gasping for breath in the privacy of his now sumptuous office.

But the worst was still to come. In November 1965, Linda announced out of the blue that she was leaving him, at least temporarily, and going to New York to see a marriage counselor. "I want to think over a lot of things," she said. "I'm not even sure now that we've got a future together."

Millard was speechless. He had been warned a year earlier that trouble was brewing when Linda had told him she didn't love him anymore, but now for the first time he felt shocked enough to realize that he must do something radical if he were to keep his home from splitting up.

The long week following Linda's departure was the loneliest, most agonizing time of his life. When he arrived at work he couldn't bear to stay in his office by himself. When he arrived home—at five o'clock instead of his usual midnight—he took his children for walks and tried to play with them; he gave baths and brushed teeth. But the net result was, to his horror, that he had become a stranger in his own home.

Five days passed before Linda phoned. She did not yet want to see him, but she suggested that he join her in New York the following week.

When Millard arrived, Linda was still uncertain about what to do. The first evening together they went to Radio City Music Hall. To their surprise the title of the movie was "Never Too Late." This proved to be a comedy about a woman who had got pregnant after she thought it was too late. When they went downstairs for refreshments while waiting for the stage show, Linda suddenly broke down and began crying. Not being able to get her to stop, Millard grabbed their coats and they stumbled out into the cold November night, leaving the stage show, their orange juice, and an umbrella!

Then it happened—the turning point. First they found themselves sitting and talking on the front steps of St. Patrick's Cathedral. Then they walked some more, rather aimlessly, and ended up in the doorway of a shop just off Fifth Avenue. At last Linda faced her husband, clutched his arms, and began being absolutely honest about her disloyalties and whatever she was most ashamed of. This moved Millard to pour out his own agony and regrets. Such a confession of their betrayal of each other broke down the barrier between them and love rushed in, in a mighty wave. As they clung to each other, the tears flowed down both their cheeks.

When they finally got back to the hotel, sleep seemed impossible. Instead, they spent all night talking, praying, and even singing. An old gospel hymn, "We're Marching to Zion," filled their minds and souls. And they felt a strong sense of the presence of God as they talked about the new direction they felt guided to take in the future. To prepare for this new life, whatever it might turn out to be, they decided that they should leave the business world, sell their interests, and give all their money away.

The following morning, as they emerged from their hotel, Millard impulsively hailed a taxi, the driver of which, instead of driving off, turned around and with a big smile on his face said, "Congratulations!"

"Congratulations? For what?" Millard asked.

"This is a brand-new cab and you are my first passengers!" came the answer.

Millard looked at Linda and saw she was already again crying.

"Driver," he said, "take us through Central Park. I've got a story to tell you."

As they wound their way around the park, Millard leaned his arms on the back of the front seat and poured out the story of what they had just experienced the night before. He ended by saying that they had decided to change the course of their lives and "start serving God." For his part the taxi driver, obviously deeply moved himself, said that he believed that his picking them up that morning was a confirmation of God's blessing and a sign that they had made exactly the right decision.

Two days later the Fullers experienced another clear sign. They were at the Kennedy Airport, waiting to board a plane for Montgomery, Alabama, when a young African in long flowing robes took a seat near them. They had already been talking about the possibility of going to Africa after all, so he interested them greatly. "You know I'd like to talk to that fellow," Millard whispered.

Encouraged by Linda, he got up, walked over to the African, and said, "Hello. Welcome to America."

"Hello," replied the other in crisp British English, explaining that he had just arrived from Nigeria and his name was Daniel Offiong. He said he was on his way to Miles College in Alabama, where he had been awarded a scholarship.

A few minutes later they all boarded the same plane and Millard felt as strong a desire to talk as he had had with the taxi driver. This was made easy, for they had been assigned space near to one another, and shortly after the plane took off the Fullers were able to move to seats immediately adjacent to their new African acquaintance.

"How much American money have you got?" Millard began.

The African pulled out a wad of traveler's checks and handed them over. "That's it," he said. "Is it much?"

There was just eighty dollars. "It won't go far in our inflated currency," Millard said. "How are you fixed for clothing? Have you got anything warm?"

"No. I'm afraid not. I only have the kind of clothes we wear in Nigeria."

Millard turned to his wife. "Have you got a checkbook in your purse?" he asked. And when Linda nodded her head, he went on, "Please draw a check for fifty dollars. That will give our friend something towards a winter overcoat."

The African student took the check and laid it on his lap and just gazed at it. After a few minutes he unbuckled his seatbelt and stood up. Then he turned to the Fullers and bowed deeply, from the waist, to each of them in turn. Sitting down he continued to look at the check. Finally rather emotionally he said, "Yesterday, before leaving home, I visited my home church and my minister told me that on reaching America I would meet a good Samaritan who would help me and see me through my needs." Tears welled up in his eyes. "This prophecy has already come true."

A few months later Daniel transferred to Tougaloo College in Jackson, Mississippi. There he had a brilliant college career and before returning home even received his doctorate degree.

In the middle 1960s Millard undertook a financial campaign to raise funds for Tougaloo College. He worked out of an office in New York and spoke frequently, giving the story of his recent spiritual rebirth at Marble Collegiate Church, at a Faith at Work meeting, and wherever he was invited to talk.

After considerable success in this work, he resigned and moved with Linda to Koinonia, a communal farm operated by Clarence Jordan, a southern gentleman, and a few friends in Americus, Georgia. (The Greek word *koinonia* means "community" or "fellowship.") Jordan's learning and wisdom and Millard's experience in sales-promotion formed two sides of a coin. A practical ministry was launched to build houses for many poor people of that area, using "biblical economics," something very different from what Millard had used in business. Houses were sold at no profit, and no interest was charged on loans. Millard and Clarence made a great team, and teamwork, after all, often forms the heart-beat of a spiritual advance.

The Fullers discovered further personal freedom and a chance to express their new outlook on life in very creative ways. In his first month at Koinonia in

1965, Millard had transacted, largely over the phone, much of the business necessary to liquidate his assets and distribute his wealth, giving it to those charitable institutions he felt he should aid.

Before long Millard and Linda visited Africa. There they became deeply concerned with a Block and Sand project to help Africans build homes in Mbandaka, the capital of what is now the equator region of Zaire. Somewhat later they returned there a second time and, with the further experience learned at Koinonia Farm in building adequate housing for the destitute, began their great, ongoing work of Habitat for Humanity which has become a new, highly effective Christian missionary undertaking in many parts of the world, including many locations in the United States. The slogan of this fast-growing work is well expressed in these twelve words "A Decent House in a Decent Community for God's People in Need."

CHAPTER TEN

The Story of A.A.'s Bill Wilson

BY IRVING HARRIS

When asked who he was, Bill would sometimes say, "Oh, just another guy who's one drink away from the gutter."

The truth about alcoholics, as he came to see it, was just as simple as that. In his Gramercy Park days, long before he and "Doctor Bob" were sweating out their famous Twelve Steps in Akron, Ohio, the sobriety which Bill found, and maintained for the remaining thirty years of his life, had a kind of New Testament directness as its very cornerstone.

As a boy in Vermont, Bill's slight tendency to gawkiness and stabs of inferiority prodded him into teenage success. He early developed a fierce determination to win, and before leaving school he had become captain of his high school baseball team as well as leader of the school's orchestra. For three years he studied engineering, then enlisted in the 66th Coast Artillery, soon after America entered World War I. He went to France among the select, as a

Reprinted from *The Breeze of the Spirit* by Irving Harris (Seabury Press, 1978).

second lieutenant from the army's Plattsburgh (New York) training camp, but not before discovering the liberating effects of a little social drinking. On his return he gravitated to Wall Street with what he refers to as a rather high opinion of himself. With little hesitation or direction, he plunged into various activities connected with the world of high finance. He took a law course at night and for awhile worked as an investigator for a surety company. On a motorcycle, with his wife, Lois, in a blue sidecar, he toured the Northeast, making confidential reports on the status of various small business enterprises. The drive for success was on.

Inevitably, Bill became involved in the stock market itself; business and financial leaders were his heroes. For several years Wall Street brought him money and applause. He and his charming Lois made an everwidening circle of friends, and their style of living left nothing to be desired—superficially, that is. But all along, drinking was assuming a more important place, soon continuing all day and frequently most of the night. His friends and his young wife remonstrated. But many around him were getting rich, so "why not I?" thought Bill, liquor and all.

Then abruptly in October 1929, all hell broke loose on the New York Stock Exchange and the effect on Bill proved catastrophic. Here's the picture as he used to tell it at Gramercy Park:

After a seething day he would wobble from brokerage office to hotel bar and back again and find the ticker-tape still chattering tardily about eight. Grabbing a strip, he would stare at an inch which read ABC–19. It might have been 54 that morning. Like most of his friends, he was soon finished. The evening papers were reporting more than one instance of a Wall Street leader's hurling himself to death from some "tower of high finance," but such cowardice disgusted Bill. Tomorrow was another day. When he was drinking again at a bar, the old fierce determination to win always came back with overwhelming force.

One morning he phoned a friend in Montreal. Apparently there was still plenty of money in Canada, and by the following spring Lois and he were living north of the border and again in their accustomed style.

For awhile Bill felt like Napoleon freed from Elba, but not for long. On his travels his drinking problem stuck right with him. One generous friend after another had to let him go, and quite soon the Wilsons were again living in Brooklyn and broke. This time they stayed broke.

They found sanctuary with Lois's parents, and Lois took a job as a salesgirl in a Manhattan department store, often reaching home exhausted to find Bill dead drunk. As for Bill, he had become an unwilling hanger-on in brokerage offices. He also loitered more and more at home where the liquor, which from a luxury had turned into a necessity, cost less. Remorse, hopelessness, even horror marked the next several years. His old courage to do battle had evaporated. Eating little or nothing when drinking, Bill was soon forty pounds underweight.

One short respite came after a visit to a nationally known New York hospital for the rehabilitation of alcoholics. He had been sent there through the interest of his brother-in-law, a physician. A kind doctor, William D. Silkworth, who became his life-long friend, not only explained how seriously ill he was but how (and why) his will power had become incapable of combating liquor. Bill felt that this partially excused his incredible behavior, so he returned to the Street and was soon making a little money again. But self-knowledge alone failed miserably to answer his problems, and the awful days of the drinking bouts returned all too soon. His family saw the undertaker or an asylum ahead, and Bill's loneliness turned into despair.

Meanwhile, on Gramercy Park, along with much personal work on personal counseling, various forces, including Sam Shoemaker's keen interest in programs for laymen, had encouraged the formation of midweek men's meetings, characteristic of A First Century Christian Fellowship, or The Oxford Group, as this movement was now being called. In many of these weekly groups Christ's promise to His followers, that where two or three of them might gather in His name, He would personally be present, was being fulfilled. The meetings were lively and spiritually effective. The one held late in the afternoon every Thursday used an attractive, conveniently located lounge on the second floor of "61" and was presided over by an experienced member of the Calvary [Church] staff, or a leader in the wider fellowship, who knew the kind of questions businessmen and wage earners needed to air and discuss: answers to pressure, personal hang-ups, honesty in competitive business dealings, fear, or unemployment.

In God's own time and through a friend's rather casual visit to this group, the first gleam of hope was relayed to Bill. One bleak November afternoon Bill's phone rang. His old boarding-school friend and drinking companion, Ebby Thatcher, was on the other end of the wire. What surprised Bill was not so much that Ebby was in town but that he was sober, and when he arrived at the family residence in Brooklyn, he seemed strangely different from the hopeless man Bill had known. On the kitchen table stood a crock of pineapple juice and gin. Bill filled a glass and pushed it across as they sat down opposite each other. But smilingly, Ebby refused.

Bill wondered what it was all about, but not for long. "I've got religion," volunteered Ebby without the slightest inhibition.

"Oh, not that!" Bill gulped a double mouthful of his brew. Then he sat glumly thinking there was nothing he could do but let his friend rant. Instead, Ebby related a short, moving story about two friends who, interceding in his favor several months before, had persuaded a New England judge to suspend sentence on a conviction in a case resulting from a brawl. They had professed faith in him, come up with a specific program of action—and it had worked.

Bill pretended to be unimpressed, but the story and especially Ebby's smile spoke to him eloquently. After all, he had always claimed to believe in a Power greater than himself. "What do you call this brand of religion?" he heard himself asking.

Ebby pretended to be tantalizingly vague. He mentioned an old church down in Gramercy Park and the friendliness shown him by men who met there week by week. "They're a great crowd," he added, "with some fresh ideas. They admit alcohol has 'em licked, so why shouldn't I? As one of them put it, 'Love's blind but the neighbors ain't!' When I took stock of myself the result was awful, but when I spilled the beans, confidentially, to another souse, I felt like a new man. I also got some helpful thoughts about making a bit of what they call 'restitution.' I was told that there was no pricetag on giving—if it's just giving yourself. And again it worked.''

This time Bill, his long legs stretched out across the kitchen floor, was silent.

Ebby didn't stay long and he had no clincher, but he spoke seriously about a new experiment in prayer with which he was now starting every day. ''Free as the air, too, Bill,'' he said, ''because you only have to pray to God *as you think He is.*''

What could be fairer than that? Bill got the distinct impression that his friend was no longer fighting a drinking problem. No, the desire to imbibe had somehow just been lifted and he was asking daily for the power, not to struggle against alcohol but to live a life. Obviously he was finding it.

For several days Bill continued to mix his gin and fruit juice, but he simply couldn't forget Ebby, not for a single moment. He felt rocked and stunned, but rather happily so. Ebby had not talked down to him nor given much advice. He felt the closeness of the old days in a fresh way. As he put it later, here was the kinship of common suffering and the enormously powerful influence of the simple fact of *one alcoholic talking to another.*

Viewed in the golden retrospect of the years to come this amounted to ''round one'' in Bill's fight for freedom.

In making him rector, Calvary Church had put several unexpected assets into Sam Shoemaker's hands, and none that he was to value more than a mission for down-and-outs on East Twenty-third Street. Connected with it was a rooming house called the Olive Tree Inn. Presided over by Harry Hadley and "Tex" Francisco, Calvary Mission provided evening meetings and simple meals, a place to sleep and, for those who were finding freedom from liquor, a warm fellowship for hopeless men. Since he totally lacked resources, Ebby had gone there to live. With the men he met, and with the new friends in nearby Gramercy Park, he now enjoyed an ever-increasing number of close relationships.

Bill knew where Ebby was and one day, between his mood swings and while still "pretty maudlin," he got the bright idea of doing a bit of religious investigation by paying Ebby a call. Unfortunately, it was a long walk from the nearest subway station to Calvary Mission and Bill began stopping in bars as he traveled east on Twenty-third Street. Most of the afternoon slipped by between drinks, and he was in high fettle in a drunken way by the time he finally reached the mission's front door. He had picked up a Finnish sailmaker and this unruly pair were on the point of being refused admission when Ebby himself appeared, quickly appraised the situation and suggested a plate of beans. After the food had been washed down with copious cups of black coffee, the newcomers heard there would shortly be a meeting in the mission hall. Would they like to go? Certainly, they said, that was why they were there.

Sitting on one of the hard wooden pews that filled the hall, Bill shivered at the sight of the derelict audience. There followed a few hymns and prayers and then an exhortation by Tex, the evening's leader. Only Jesus could save, he said, and strangely enough his words failed to jar Bill. Whatever he meant, Bill felt he must be right. He listened with rising excitement as certain men got up and gave testimonials. Then came "the call." As various men started forward, Bill found himself unaccountably motivated, heading for the altar. Ebby grabbed for his coattails but it was too late. Bill knelt, shaking the more, among the penitents and felt, perhaps for the first time, truly penitent himself. He had a wild impulse to talk and this he soon did with deep earnestness and in a way that compelled attention.

Afterwards, sitting in the dormitory in the building next door, where Ebby was living, he could remember scarcely a word he had said. Ebby, obviously relieved, told him he had done all right and had "given his life to God."

This experience may be called "round two."

When he reached home Bill gave a full account of his experience to Lois, and they had a long and earnest talk. It seemed significant to both of them that on his return trip along Twenty-third Street he had never once thought of going into a bar. This was something very new!

Came the dawn, and Bill realized that he had slept like a baby and without an ounce of gin. He had only a slight hangover, not the devastating head he had expected. But his old habits still gripped him. He would not be a fanatic about this new life. He would take another drink or two just by way of tapering off.

When Lois had left for work, the process became easier, and instead of tapering off he took a couple more and nicely succeeded in tapering on. At six o'clock his wife found him upstairs on the bed and, of course, drunk.

So it went for two grim days, but Ebby's smile and the mission experience never left him. On the morning of the third day his wandering thoughts gathered into a sharp focus as he began to compare himself to a victim of cancer. Surely if he had cancer he would not sit at home and put cold cream on the affected parts. Certainly not! He would look up the best doctor in the business and put himself unreservedly into his hands. So now he would return to the hospital and his old friend Dr. Silkworth. Here at least he would be helped to sober up, and then perhaps he could take a fresh look at Ebby's formula for sobriety.

He arrived at the hospital in wretched shape, having consumed two bottles of beer en route. According to all accounts, Dr. Silkworth met him in the hall. In very high spirits Bill waved a third bottle in the doctor's face, and yelled, "At last, Doc, I've found something!" At this the good doctor's face fell, and Bill realized all the more how deeply the medical man loved him. The doctor merely shook his head and intimated that it might be time for Bill to get upstairs and into bed.

Some three days passed. The effects of both the alcohol and the sedatives he had been given wore off. In their place Bill suffered a dull sense of emptiness and depression. As he put it, he was "still choking on the God business." Then, bright and early one morning he saw Ebby's smiling face before him again,

Ebby in person. Ah, thought Bill, here's where he thinks he's going to evangelize me. He waited suspiciously but nothing happened except that Ebby entered the room and sat down.

Finally it was Bill who spoke. "What's that neat little formula once more?" he asked. In perfect good humor Ebby recited the group precepts again. You admit you are licked. You get honest with yourself. You talk things out with somebody else. If possible you make restitution to the people you have harmed. You try to give of yourself without stint and with no demand for reward. And you pray to whatever God you think there is, entirely as an experiment. It was as simple and as mysterious as that.

After some small talk, Ebby again vanished. Bill's depression deepened unbearably. It seemed to him as though he were now at the very bottom of the pit. He still gagged badly on the notion of approaching that "Power greater than yourself," but the last vestige of his pride and obstinacy had been crushed.

Then quite suddenly he found himself crying out, "If there is a God, let Him show himself. I am ready to do anything, *anything!*"

At this the whole room lit up with a great light reminiscent of the Spirit of Christmas Present in Dickens's *A Christmas Carol.* Bill could only describe it by saying that he had been caught up in an ecstasy. In his mind's eye he saw himself on the top of a high mountain with the wind of the Spirit blowing. The acute sense that burst upon him that he was a free man was crucial.

This proved to be his third and in a sense his final "round."

Slowly his ecstasy subsided, and instead he felt a great peace and a presence that he could only identify as the supernatural Presence of the Living God. No matter how terrible the past had been, of one thing he was sure—the future was to be all right for it was to be with Him.

When Dr. Silkworth next stopped in, Bill tried to give him an account of his astonishing experience. He feared the doctor might feel that he was hallucinating or losing his mind. But the reverse proved to be the doctor's attitude. He immediately encouraged Bill to hold on to the reality of all he had gone through. "You're by no means going crazy," he said. "Some basic psychological or spiritual event has happened. Hang on to it. Anything is better than the way you were."

Then faithful Ebby called again, this time with a worn copy of *The Varieties of Religious Experience* by the great Harvard psychologist William James. Together they devoured parts of it. Spiritual experiences, James had written, were gifts from the blue but they could transform people. Often they were preceded by pain, suffering, or calamity. Complete hopelessness and "deflation at depth" were almost always part of the picture. Bill took it all personally, for this was his own history, especially the realization that "deflation at depth" had ushered in the spiritual renewal and freedom he now felt.

Before the day was out he was already focused on changing the world and when he was dismissed from the hospital, he started out after drunks like a person on jet propulsion. He envisioned a chain reaction that would dry up the nation. But actually his next necessary lesson was the old adage that patience is a virtue.

As part of the new life, he threw himself into group activity both at Calvary House and Calvary Mission. He took on alcoholics, by the score; some would clear up for a little while but then flop dismally. Bill maintained his own sobriety, however, but at the end of six months nobody else had become sober for long. Unfortunately he wasn't meeting men at their own point of need, as Ebby had done for him. Instead he was trying to impose Robert E. Speer's four "absolute standards" from the Sermon on the Mount. These standards, that had often been used so wisely by Oxford Group leaders and others on people who were physically sick and mentally obsessed, were now backfiring.

Dr. Silkworth was one of the first to underline Bill's mistaken approach. "You're *preaching* at these fellows, Bill," he said, in essence, "although no one ever preached at you. Turn your strategy around. Remember Professor James's insistence that 'deflation at depth' is the foundation of most spiritual experiences like your own. Give your new contacts the *medical* business—and hard. Describe the obsession that condemns men to drink and the physical sensitivity or allergy of the body that makes this type go mad or die if they keep on drinking."

Bill saw the point and heartily agreed. However, not a little pressure continued to be brought on him by some of his new friends who wanted him to forget his alcoholics and get on with "changing the world." For his part, Bill knew that he was being called to go for something more specific, and that more than anything else he wanted to work with alcoholics. In this Sam Shoemaker remained a staunch ally, for despite his immersion in both group and parish work,

Sam well remembered his own signal failure with the few drunks to whom he had given rooms in Calvary House instead of at the Olive Tree Inn. Who could forget? One of these had gleefully tossed an alarm clock out of a fourth floor window in the dead of night, putting it neatly through a stained glass window of the church. At early communion the next morning the clergy had suddenly noticed it on the embroidered cloth of the high altar. Sam realized further that the pull on Bill to work with others who were handicapped as he had been represented something very special. While he remained just as unclear as Bill as to where and how this "ministry" would finally take root, he strongly shared Bill's desire to explore his true vocation and look for an open door through which he might fulfill it.

Strangely enough Bill's chance came not in New York City but among another crowd of Oxford Group friends in Akron, Ohio. In looking for work Bill had drifted back to Wall Street again, still completely sober but very frustrated. One day, through a chance acquaintance in a brokerage office, he got himself mixed up in a proxy-fight involving a small manufacturing company in the Midwest. He and a few others visited Ohio to look into things. Again in fine fettle, Bill could already see himself as the company's new president, but when the chips were down the other side had more proxies and Bill and his friends got ousted.

At this point everyone but Bill returned to New York. With no more than ten dollars in his pocket, he found himself at the Mayflower Hotel in Akron on the eve of Mother's Day—and alone. As he paced the hotel lobby he could see the bar filling up at one end and hear the familiar buzz of conversation mounting. But God was with him. He recalled clearly that it had always been *by trying to help other alcoholics* that he had stayed sober himself. That was it, he thought. He must find another alcoholic to talk to. Down deep he realized for the first time that he needed that other alcoholic just as much as the man he wanted to help needed him.

Across from the bar at the far end of the lobby he paused by a church directory. Then quite at random he called an Episcopal priest and to his listener's amazement poured out his tale. Finally he asked if the minister knew of someone who could put him in touch with another alcoholic. When the good man realized what Bill was looking for, he may well have envisioned two people getting drunk instead of one. In any event he finally got Bill's point and came up with a list of some ten people who might be able to help.

Still in the phone booth Bill began calling. It was a Saturday afternoon and scarcely anyone was home. One line was busy and the few people who did answer failed to respond. Bill got down to the very last name, but this one call did the trick. A young married woman, Henrietta Seiberling, answered. She had no drinking problem herself, she said, but she knew a man, a doctor, who indeed did need help. She suggested that Bill come straight over and pursue things further.

So it was that within twenty-four hours Bill stood face to face with "Dr. Bob" who, with his wife, Anne, had gone to several group meetings in Akron, and who was later to become A.A. member number two and cofounder with Bill of Alcoholics Anonymous.

Nothing seemed very promising at the time. Dr. Bob and Anne came in. The doctor, visibly shaking, explained that he could only stay for a minute. However, their hostess discreetly led the two men to a small library and there they went on talking until after eleven o'clock at night. Bill kept reminding himself that previously, in New York, his aggressive approach had backfired, so he proceeded carefully, with no mention of the fireworks of his own full-blown religious experience. He bore down on an alcoholic's allergy to liquor and his obsession with drink once he got started. Though Dr. Bob was a medical doctor this was news to him, *bad* news. But here they were, two drunks, face-to-face, and one of them with an answer. This mutual give-and-take became the very heart of A.A. in the days to come. As Bill talked the doctor relaxed. "Yes, that's me," he began. "I'm like that." They were talking the same language.

As it worked out, Bill went to live with Dr. Bob and Anne. Every morning they experimented in having their devotions together. As Bill described it later, Anne would sit in the corner by the fireplace and read from the Bible, and then they would huddle together in the stillness awaiting inspiration and guidance. The final missing link in Bill's program had been located, and new insights were given. Both men felt the immense importance of continuing to work with other alcoholics and, through contacts at the Akron City Hospital, the third and fourth members of A.A. were reached, helped, and included in their fellowship.

101

Besides that first Akron group, on Bill's return East, there soon developed a weekly meeting in the Wilsons' Brooklyn parlor. When Bill visited Sam Shoemaker, who had been keenly following the program, the two had a memorable reunion. After a few months, several meeting places opened up, such as a room in New York Steinway Hall, one in a Manhattan tailoring shop, and others in suburban homes. Gradually groups began to appear in other cities—Philadelphia, Washington, Baltimore, and Cleveland. An A.A. ferment had begun to work and the good news began to spread rapidly. Today every city in the land and hundreds overseas—one might say almost every hamlet—has its A.A. group. And the end is never in sight. For alcoholism has become a major illness throughout the world. Praise God that, through the faithfulness and experience of two men, this growing problem has an answer—adequate, effective, and immediately at hand.

The Twelve Steps of Alcoholics Anonymous*

According to Lois Wilson, when Bill was writing the "big" A.A. book in 1938, he thought of his many talks with Dr. Bob about the importance of stressing the spiritual aspect of the program. He therefore expanded the original six steps, which they had learned from the Oxford Group, into the famous Twelve Steps now used around the world. He had a deep desire to make it impossible for an alcoholic who wanted sobriety to find a single loophole. The steps have never since been altered.

*Reprinted with permission of A.A. World Services, Inc., copyright owners, P.O. Box 459, Grand Central Station, New York, N.Y. 10017.

Step One: We admitted that we were powerless over alcohol—that our lives had become unmanageable.

Step Two: Came to believe that a Power greater than ourselves could restore us to sanity.

Step Three: Made a decision to turn our will and our lives over to the care of God *as we understand Him.*

Step Four: Made a searching and fearless moral inventory of ourselves.

Step Five: Admitted to God, to ourselves, and to another human being the exact nature of our wrongs.

Step Six: Were entirely ready to have God remove all these defects of character.

Step Seven: Humbly asked Him to remove our shortcomings.

Step Eight: Made a list of all persons we had harmed and became willing to make amends to them all.

Step Nine: Made direct amends to such people whenever possible, except when to do so would injure them or others.

Step Ten: Continued to take personal inventory and when we were wrong promptly admitted it.

Step Eleven: Sought through prayer and meditation to improve our conscious contact with God *as we understood Him,* praying only for knowledge of His will for us and the power to carry that out.

Step Twelve: Having had a spiritual awakening as the result of these steps, we tried to carry this message to alcoholics and to practice these principles in all our affairs.

CHAPTER ELEVEN

Disinherited

ALYS BOROSS SMITH

This is the story of a young woman who chose the uncertainties of a life of fellowship and action to the comforts of a Park Avenue apartment. Alys Boross Smith was born in Vienna of a Hungarian father and an American mother who met aboard a trans-Atlantic steamer. Her mother, on a previous journey just before the turn of the century, had been courted by the famous Italian scientist Marconi, who was in the midst of experiments leading to the invention of wireless telegraphy. On that earlier trip, through her mother's influence with the ship's captain, Marconi made his first successful ship-to-shore experiments. Alys's mother and Marconi were nearly married when the bride-to-be broke the engagement, and for a very important reason—Marconi's father threatened to withhold his financial backing if his son married an American. At this news the betrothed ended the relationship, feeling that purely personal plans should not be allowed to interfere with the consummation of what she believed to be the inventor's God-given talent.

Thus it transpired that the same beautiful American girl, on a second ocean crossing, once again became involved in an affair of the heart. This time the suitor was a dashing Hungarian who was to become Alys's father. He pursued his beloved all over Europe and finally the young people got engaged, appropriately enough, in a gondola in Venice. Soon after, they were married in an Anglican church in London and, following a short time in Budapest, settled in Vienna where Alys's older sister, Gene, and she were both born. Then in 1906 the mother's homesickness for her own country and the father's love of America brought about a move to Larchmont, New York, where they lived during most of the time when the girls were growing up. Shortly before Alys was ready for college, the family took a Park Avenue apartment in New York City. The home was filled with paintings by Old Masters and fully staffed and, furthermore, operated under the rule of a man with a tight hand who expected implicit obedience on the part of his children.

Alys's proficiency as a scholar made it possible for her to enter the same class as her sister in Bryn Mawr College. Nothing in their previous religious experience had meant very much, so that college, while it offered a refreshing personal freedom in contrast to their strict home life in New York, added no special vitality to their personal faith.

But spiritual gifts lay straight ahead. Alys says that there were actually four stages in her conversion. *The first stage* she calls "Turned on to God." This started with a period of "sermon-tasting." She was exposed to numerous talks about Christianity at Bryn Mawr but none of these really touched her. She realized vaguely that some very important element was lacking in her life, and she had a sense of groping for it. "Being intellectual" next became the thing for her to go for. Breakfast parties with new friends were thus a substitute for regular church attendance. She continued to be very self-conscious because of being rather tall, and her shyness when speaking in classroom work convinced her that she must be very stupid. Fortunately, in the long run, this sense of inadequacy was partially compensated for by her participation in amateur theatricals. She got one of the leading roles in a Gilbert and Sullivan operetta, but this proved only a partial answer to her small sense of self-worth.

Her second stage in conversion she calls "Turned over to God." This happened during her senior year when she had the opportunity to be one of two classmates to represent Bryn Mawr at a student religious conference at Princeton. Her principal motive in going, she admits, was that the conference offered her a chance to meet some college boys—perhaps the last chance she would have for a long time because of the strict home life she knew she would be subject to in New York after graduation.

The first gathering at the conference turned out to be a friendly dinner meeting, and right across the table from her sat a Princeton graduate, Donald Carruthers, the chaplain to Presbyterian students at Penn State College. An attractive fellow, he had much to say about "the romance of the Christian religion" and was the first person ever to talk to Alys about Jesus Christ, assuring her that Christ could transform a person's life. He also described prayer as a practical power that could guide an individual in every aspect of daily life. He urged her to start a prayer fellowship among a few of her friends back at college and promised to come and speak to a group of students there in the near future.

Alys was intrigued, and the very night she returned to college she felt convinced that she must take a plunge into the unknown. Like a child, she knelt down by her bed and with the prayer, "Lord, my Father, take me," she handed her life over to God. As Sam Shoemaker once expressed it, she committed as much of herself as she could to as much of God as she understood. And something important happened. Basically the step represented letting go of her own will. She had no deep emotional feelings, but in her heart she knew that she had "come home."

The next day the campus and everyone about her looked quite different. Whereas she had been spiritually blind, she realized now that she saw with new eyes and had been given a new direction with clear goals. She had made a real turnabout and her life would be concerned with God's will for her rather than with merely her own selfish plans.

The third stage in her conversion she calls "Turned unto God as Savior." Thus far Jesus had always been for her a Jesus of history, a rather shadowy figure whom she did not know intimately at all. Now she suddenly realized that He could mean a great deal more.

This came to a focus at a meeting of college girls in Yonkers, New York, soon after her graduation. The meeting was led by Sam Shoemaker who had recently become rector of Calvary Episcopal Church, New York. At the first meeting she attended, the speaker was a brand-new Christian, Jewish by

107

background and lately graduated from Dartmouth, who told the story of his own start on the road to faith. His honesty impressed Alys greatly. At another meeting Sam offered a helpful definition of sin; he said that it was "anything that keeps you from God or from another person." Wow! What about that lifelong sense of inferiority and her continuing fear of a dominating Hungarian father? She was also aware of a negative way in which she had been constantly comparing herself with her older sister. In a breakthrough she saw that Jesus as Savior could free her from all of these heavy burdens if she would but hand them over to Him *and not snatch them back*. As she did this, she had a clear sense that Jesus Christ was alive and that His gift of the Holy Spirit was in truth His presence within her, a living reality forever. When sin recurred she clearly understood what to do with it in order to keep the channel clear. So she determined that she would no longer be enslaved by attitudes that had created her self-centeredness.

Her fourth step in conversion she calls "Turned out to others." She had made a start in this direction in her college prayer group. There, with a few other classmates including her sister, she had first, in fear and trembling, prayed out loud. There she had also understood more and more that following the Christian way was by no means a "solo experience" but rather an experience of fellowship modeled on the relationship which Jesus had first formed with His own disciples. Studying His life, she realized that what Americans called teamwork would have to remain central in everything she did.

Soon after graduation Alys took a job as a social caseworker, which expressed her desire to help people.

She became a volunteer caseworker in a large social-service organization and under careful supervision she became involved with six slum families. Thus she was soon dealing with individuals' accidents, family problems, and in such questions as naturalization.

At the same time greatly wanting to please her father she tried to identify with his interest in Old Masters and other paintings by taking courses at the Metropolitan Museum of Art. She also knew that he expected women to know something about business, so she read numerous volumes about stocks and bonds. She never had a dull moment and loved all of her activities.

Despite her best efforts, however, trouble soon developed. Her father, for instance, strongly disapproved of her visits to poor families on the East Side and convinced himself that, unprotected, his daughter stood a good chance of being stabbed and robbed. He forbade her continuing such work. Alys felt heartbroken and for a time had no answer to what to do with her time. Then a clerical friend named Leslie Glenn, who was heading up College Work for the National Episcopal Church, found her a job at the Episcopal Church headquarters in the department of Religious Education. Alys first acted as assistant librarian, but before long she found herself Information Receptionist for the entire building and at times was allowed to travel in order to speak to college students who were interested in religion. She had by no means forgotten her commitment to teamwork, so she came up with a plan for department heads and the secretarial staff to meet regularly for prayer and fellowship, and this blossomed most successfully.

Meanwhile her sister had found an opening close by in the work of Calvary Church parish where she organized courses in religious education.

Alas, such activities again came to grief. Arriving home one evening she found her sister deeply upset. Their father objected to all that both the girls were doing and this time had come up with an ultimatum: they would have to choose between their new work and loyalty to him. In fact if they did not choose occupations more in line with his interests, they would have to leave home and be disinherited.

The sisters took almost a month thinking and praying about this crisis and then with the help of Sam Shoemaker decided to leave home. With very few belongings they moved to rooms owned and operated by the Calvary Church vestry and when Calvary House opened on Gramercy Park, they were allocated to one of the newly available double rooms in that soon-to-be-famous parish center.

As far as their father was concerned, the result was prompt and drastic. For two months he sent his daughters fifty dollars but then disinherited them. Even their letters were unanswered and when, a short time later, in a double ceremony, the girls married two clergymen who worked on the Calvary Church staff, he moved back to Budapest himself, abandoning New York entirely. The sole communication came in the form of hostile letters to his sons-in-law filled with anger and resentment.

It is not in the province of this chapter to outline the spiritually fruitful and useful life Alys found with her husband "Jack" Smith, or to describe the notable ministry they both found heading up All Saints' Church in Beverly Hills, California. But we must round out Alys's relationship with her father by saying that after several years and in what all concerned felt to be a miraculous answer to constant prayer, a most happy reconciliation took place. By the time two grandsons had appeared, the father returned briefly to America loaded with honors from the Hungarian government. He allowed himself to be persuaded by the family attorney to see his new families, and one day he actually visited them at Gramercy Park. It turned out to be a new day of overwhelming joy and, believe it or not, all was forgiven.

CHAPTER TWELVE

A Jewish Businessman
Discovers the Messiah

JOSEPH KLUTCH

Among the crowds who used to come to the open meetings at Calvary House on Thursday nights was a Jewish manufacturer whose grandparents had migrated to the United States from Russia. While his grandparents conscientiously observed the traditional rabbinical customs and Holy Days, Judaism had very little meaning for Joe Klutch. When people asked him if he believed in God, Joe would answer yes, but actually God was anything but real. In fact it seemed downright silly to him to think of the Creator of the universe caring about anyone as insignificant as himself.

Like many others, as his business grew, he became involved in worldly pleasures—drinking, gambling, playing around—the works. He lived in a cosmopolitan neighborhood and happened to have an Italian family on one side and an Irish family on the other as immediate neighbors. Joe noticed that members of these households wore crosses and called themselves Christians, but there were signs that basically they hated Jews and thus the cross seemed rather like a threat.

112

Though his business was prospering, after a time Joe discovered that his patent attorney was a crook. The lawyer was pocketing the appropriate fees but completely neglecting to register the patents for Joe's products. Fortunately he received a letter from another patent attorney, Willis Rice, who had an official connection with New York City and was apparently honest. Willis tracked down a number of unregistered patents and got the authorization to return these to their rightful owners, and out of this happy circumstance there sprang up a warm friendship. Joe's trademarks were properly registered and Mr. Rice also offered the manufacturer more than a little invaluable counsel on some new products which the latter was bringing out. When the attorney discovered that Joe was Jewish but without any vital faith, he even took an interest in his spiritual welfare.

One day Joe received a card, obviously sent at Willis Rice's suggestion, inviting him to an evening meeting in New York City at which, it was announced, several businessmen would be speaking about faith from their own experience. The meeting was called "Faith at Work." In his entire life Joe had never once entered a church. Furthermore, he was both a shy and a rather proud person. He didn't make friends easily and in the main felt rather superior to the average person. However, he appreciated Mr. Rice's concern and so, rather reluctantly, he finally decided to go to the meeting.

On the appointed night Joe was late in reaching Calvary House, the place of the meeting, which he found to be a brick building adjoining an old brownstone church on East 21st Street. The big door seemed strangely forbidding and it took him a good

113

fifteen minutes to summon the courage to go ahead in. When he did enter, he was surprised to find a roomful of people in a brightly lighted hall, all smiling. One man stepped forward and grasped Joe's hand, saying that his name was Ralston Young. Joe had never seen a gathering before which seemed to radiate so much love. He thought he must be dreaming.

As he took a seat he heard a man telling a story about finding personal freedom from alcohol by associating with those in Faith at Work and by "surrendering his life to Jesus Christ." It all seemed a bit childish and Joe especially disliked the word *surrender*. At this point the leader of the meeting took over and to Joe's astonishment remarked that he was a Jew named Bernie Gair. He went on to say that he taught in a Brooklyn high school and recently had come to see that Jesus Christ was no less than the Messiah, "the chosen one" proclaimed in the Scriptures, "the Redeemer of all mankind." Joe was thoroughly shocked by such a statement and wanted nothing so much now as to get home and forget about the meeting completely. On the subway ride back to Brooklyn he had the comforting thought that, after all, he would never see any of these Faith at Work people again. However, over the weekend he couldn't get the Gramercy Park evening out of his mind.

Monday morning arrived and Joe hopped on his usual bus on the way to work; he had only gone two blocks when to his amazement who should also board the bus but Bernie Gair—in fact he seated himself just across the aisle. This was too much for Joe's shyness and the first thing he knew he was introducing himself and explaining that he had been at the Thursday meeting. He found Bernie exceedingly friendly and after a few minutes the latter went on to describe another meeting at the same address, one for business and professional men that took place late every Monday afternoon. At first Joe's reaction was, "No, no, not for me," but Bernie was persuasive, and in the end he got Joe to promise to attend. He assured him that he could come entirely as an observer, sit on the sidelines, so to speak, and simply listen. "There will be no pressure on you whatsoever to accept anything you hear."

A week later Joe visited 61 Gramercy Park for the second time, located the men's group, and drew a chair up to the edge of the circle. He felt none too sympathetic but gradually he became interested. There were an openness and a spirit about the meeting that impressed him, and as Mondays came around he found himself looking forward to returning. Besides other businessmen like himself, he met an architect, a stockbroker, a couple of journalists, and occasionally the minister of the church. He had little to say, but each session gave him something to think about. Then, as he talked to different ones after the meetings broke up, he lost a lot of his shyness and began to understand how very practical faith in God could be. He realized that the "regulars" were praying for him and he secretly longed for the peace and love they seemed to have, but he still shrank from that word *surrender*—which to him meant defeat—and besides, he didn't want to give up his worldly pleasures.

To be honest, the more he reasoned things out, the clearer it became that, in God's sight, he was a very selfish person, dishonest as well, and foolishly bound by fear—always holding back. And in the end he came to see that mere reasoning would never get him anywhere—that faith alone was the key. His part was simply to be willing, in faith, to let God come into his heart and take over.

Finally, the moment came when he decided to trust God instead of his own wits, and let Him take control of his whole life. That was the turning point and it came after a Monday meeting—a quiet, inner decision just as he was starting home. The new quality of love for which he had been praying fairly overwhelmed him. He says it was almost like flying. In the subway he experienced nothing so much as a great compassion for the very kind of people whom he had always disliked and in some cases hated.

On reaching home, Joe told his wife that he had discovered the secret of a new and better way of life. She knew that something had been happening; quite easily she could now see that a great joy had taken possession of her husband and she began to rejoice with him. They both agreed that what Joe had experienced was like finding a cure to cancer. Surely a kind of miracle had taken place, for some of the very things he had hated he began to love and what he had once loved unwisely he began to hate. What he had found seemed worth telling to the whole world.

For the first time the Word of God in the Bible became of interest; in fact, Joe felt a hunger to read it. And of the many passages which inspired him, the following took on a very special significance: "If any man be in Christ, he is a new creature: old things are passed away; behold, all things are become new" (II Cor. 5:17).

God had become Joe's most important and lasting living reality.

CHAPTER THIRTEEN

Walking in the Light

BY NORMAN GRUBB

I had a privileged birth and upbringing.* My father was an evangelical clergyman of the Grubb family of County Tipperary and my mother one of the aristocracy of the Marquis of Bute's family of Scotland. But what really mattered was the quiet influence of a home which was both godly and harmonious—except for the disharmonies of three growing boys and their sister!

With this background I always had a kind of take-it-for-granted faith, though by the time I reached the Upper Sixth of my school, Marlborough College, I did begin to question the actual existence of God and Christ, just as every healthy young mind should, and when I was reading John Stuart Mill's *Utilitarianism*, in which even the best in this life is called "enlightened self-interest," I uncomfortably thought to myself, "That's surely true of me. Everybody is for me—and that seems wrong."

---

*Norman Grubb is the former International Secretary of Worldwide Evangelization Crusade, U.S.A., headquarters in Fort Washington, Pennsylvania, where he now lives. He served for many years with C. T. Studd in Africa.

What I needed was the shock of a direct question about my faith, and I got it from a retired British army major who had some of us boys over to his place for tennis. Getting me alone one day, he asked, "Do you belong to Christ?" This created a crisis of honesty such as occurs in the life of everyone. Of course, as a normal, embarrassed young Englishman, I could easily have escaped this question by a vague assent, but I knew I couldn't honestly say I belonged to One whose very existence I doubted. So, with just enough of what I would now call grace from God, I said no.

The whole experience proved healthily radical for me because it sent me home feeling that if I could not call Jesus Christ my Savior, I would be going straight to hell instead of to a safe haven in heaven! I was also keenly aware of my boyhood sins, and the combination of emotions sent me to my knees, in my own room, asking for forgiveness. For years I had made this request mechanically in the Lord's Prayer, but this time it was urgent and the result was revolutionary and totally life-changing—the opening of my inner eyes to an actual living Jesus who had saved me from hell by shedding His own blood for me. I realized now that God had become my Father and heaven my destiny.

Thus started a love affair which has not only never ended but mightily increased. In other words I saw the meaning of Jesus' words to Nicodemus, "You must be born again," and that only when one is "born of the Spirit," can he "see the Kingdom of God." The kind of peace and joy and love began to be mine which put right into the shade my only former love—of football.

Stage two was how the same Spirit defined the objectives of life, as well as assured my safety for the future. This had centered in the love of a girl, a good love, for the girl was in the church; but she drew back from anything as "fanatical" as a love affair with Jesus.

An agonizing three weeks for me followed, but then the Spirit faithfully struck by leading me to read a booklet and telling me, "You can't have both Christ and anti-Christ in your heart. You must only have one or the other." Radical again, but I could not escape that Voice. What God really did was to confirm which was my true love. The girl later married another, and much later still, I found the most perfect wife in the world, C. T. Studd's youngest daughter, Pauline!*

What was much more important than human marriage, however, was that my whole self, with all its interests, was now captured for life by the Eternal Spirit and His interests. At almost the same time Britain went to war. I was given a commission as a 2nd Lieutenant in the British army—which in World War I was certainly built on callow youths!—and I was shortly on my way to join my battalion for training. What I most wanted was to bring boldly to all of us who would soon be "cannon fodder" the offer of the necessity of eternal life, and I did so to both my fellow officers and men—and have never stopped doing so.

---

*C. T. Studd was a famous university cricketer who became one of the famous Cambridge Seven—seven Cambridge University men who answered the call for missionaries to China in the 1880s and joined the China Inland Mission. C. T. Studd later founded the Worldwide Evangelization Crusade in Africa.

In this crisis of total commitment I further learned the truth of Jesus' drastic teaching that it is better to lose even an eye or a hand—both very useful—than let your selfish use of them become blocks to God's true purposes for your life.

All this conditioned me so that five years later, after university, I recognized my true "military commission," namely, to take Christ to those who had never heard of Him. I was caught by the fire of C. T. Studd's all-out dedication to carry the gospel to the unreached tribes in "the heart of Africa," to whom he had gone. I joined him, taking his daughter Pauline along with me.

I still had inner-self problems—strains, wrong reactions, and an inability to handle the sudden pressure of the positives and negatives of life. My true Waterloo came with the full solution of these, beginning with a magazine sent out to us in the Congo by a friend of Pauline's. This brought us the help of a brilliant Bible teacher in Britain, Mrs. Jessie Penn Lewis, a diminutive person in stature but a giantess in the things of the Spirit. Pauline and I were visiting in a banana plantation and one night, after following through with the Scriptures for five hours, we saw Mrs. Lewis's point of saying the word of faith as given in Paul's famous declaration in Galatians 2:20 that we were now "crucified with Christ" and thus dead, in His death, to the old indwelling spirit of error, and as Paul adds, "Nevertheless I live, yet not I but Christ lives in me."

In Colossians 1:24-29, writing to those already "in the body of Christ," Paul calls this "the mystery of Christ in you" now revealed to the born-again. We realized that this was further explained in another epistle, Romans, chapters 6 through 8. As we "confessed it with our mouths," it echoed in our hearts and there came to us both in different ways the inner witness of the Spirit, "Yes, that is what you actually are now."

This became the permanent basis of our living. We were free to be, and to accept ourselves as, God's chosen vessels—branches, temples, and thus what all the redeemed are when we boldly "possess our possessions" by faith. Just as invisible electricity is seen as light through a lamp, so the redeemed become "the light of the world" if Christ is seen in us. Or as a glowing red-hot iron, He is the fire, we the iron, yet one.

Thus we understood the total key to living—we fully functioning as ourselves and yet inwardly knowing this is actually Christ expressed in us, and learning not to accept condemnations in our life's battles and frequent tensions, which are the enemy's chief weapon in disturbing the consciousness of our union relationship with Christ.

I learned a further lesson when visiting our missionary and African friends in Ruanda (now Rwanda) in East Africa. They have learned there "to keep short accounts with God." When they are conscious of anything shadowing their sense of peace and rightness with God—what they call their "cups running over"—they "walk in the light," by which they mean being honest before God. And if they are conscious of some barrier like resentment and pride, or lust or what not, they immediately make it right with God by facing and confessing the sin, thanking God for the cleansing in the blood (according to

I John 1:7 and 9) and then, in their evening fellowships, sharing one thing and another, always with the emphasis on the cleansing rather than on the sinning.

During the visit, I was conscious of an English person who had arrived on a visit and whom I had disliked—for no particular reason. The Spirit disturbed me about this and it took quite a battle for me to face it in an adequate way. I asked God's forgiveness privately in my own prayers but this proved insufficient. I had to come out with it and go to the man personally and ask his forgiveness, and at the same time seek a cleansing. Then of course my attitude changed and the ill will disappeared.

Walking in the light like that has been a great reviving means among those thousands of African Ruandas and Uganda Christians, and the missionaries with them, and I find it is healthy for us all. Roy Hession's *Calvary Road* was written about this.

So "my ways in Christ," as Paul called them, have been very simple and really commonplace, for Christ is a good leveler, and I enjoy sharing what is solely God's abounding grace in Him.

CHAPTER FOURTEEN

A Special Collection of Stories

HELEN SHOEMAKER AND OTHERS

Like many people, Helen Shoemaker* experienced the sense of God's presence long before she was converted. He was gently nudging her along the road of faith.

She grew up in the college town of Princeton, and among a number of undergraduates who came to her home one young man seemed outstanding. He possessed a quiet confidence and an inner authority that impressed her. One day she asked him to tell her frankly what he had that she didn't have, and quite frankly he said that he had found God. When she went further and inquired how this had happened, he replied, "I took hold of God by the handle of my own sins."

Scornfully Helen replied that she didn't believe in sin. But she was enough interested to ask further questions. The student then gave her a most practical definition. "Sin," he said, "is anything which stands

*Helen Shoemaker is co-founder of the Anglican Fellowship of Prayer and the widow of the Reverend Samuel Moor Shoemaker. This account is paraphrased with the author's permission from her book, *The Exploding Mystery of Prayer* (Seabury Press, 1978).

between you and other people, or between you and God, and it includes any habit or thought which you can't control."

Any number of people at once came to Helen's mind whom she disliked or criticized, or of whom she was jealous. And along with these she became aware of a measure of self-pity and inferiority, also envy and pride. All of a sudden she had a great plenty of unpleasant things to work on.

Shortly after this the undergraduate persuaded her to go to a religious conference. Helen was sure it would prove dull, but then she falsely assumed that she would merely be an observer.

Actually, soon after arrival, the same undergraduate took time to ask her a number of troublesome questions. One was, "Would you dare to give as much of yourself as you know to as much of God as you understand?" Helen asked, "You mean forever?" He answered, "Yes." And she said, "But what if God asks me to live like Saint Francis or someone else of that kind?" He replied, "What if He does? Wouldn't you like to get free of the hang-ups you now see in your life?"

After a long, frightening battle with herself, Helen said yes. She feared that many of her friends and family would think she was crazy or a fanatic. She knew that she might be asked to change her whole style of life, but she said yes, and a mysterious ecstasy flooded her whole being, the afterglow of which has stayed with her throughout her life. At that point she knew that the great God, her Creator, had claimed her for His purposes, and that step by step He would unfold them to her.

She says she was an average upper-middle-class girl with the social mores of the times, a high-school education, plenty of relational hang-ups, and an interest in art and marriage. She had no formal experience with the church. After her conversion, her Christian nurture started in small group fellowship and prayer. Four years later she married a priest of the church. She had had no experience with death, but a year later she faced the possibility of her own death at the time of the birth of her first child. She had no knowledge of what was demanded of a clergy wife, but she was a clergy wife for thirty-three years, involved in all the challenge and adventure of it. She was called upon to raise two daughters under the public scrutiny of two large congregations.

She was plunged into all the intricacies of churchmanship and Christian service and organizational responsibility and she was led to "listen" and to fast and to pray over and over and over, because without this she realized that she simply did not have the capacity to cope with it all. But in the mysterious fellowship of prayer and public worship the rough places were smoothed out and the dark places were lighted, and when she fell down, as apparently often happened, God picked her up and dusted her off and showed her what to do next. Actually her life has been unfolding like a tapestry through the fifty years of life with Him, her never-failing wonderful friend, Jesus Christ.

A Clergyman's Tale—by Walden Pell II

Before starting on this story I tried to figure out whether I was a "once born" or a "born again"

Christian, and I came to the conclusion that I was a "once-and-a-half born" Christian! See what *you* think.

Born on Long Island, I grew up in New York City where, interestingly enough to some readers, my family attended Calvary Episcopal Church. There, on the corner of what used to be 4th Avenue and 21st Street, I was baptized and confirmed, and considerably later there I took the first step in being ordained in the Protestant Episcopal Church—I became a "deacon." The Calvary rector in those days was the Reverend Theodore Sedgwick, a man of great learning, dedication, and warmth. He gave me that special feeling of really being at home in God's house.

Although Calvary was somewhat on the "low" side of the Episcopal church, I several times experienced the presence of the supernatural in the old sanctuary there—especially up in the chancel, near the altar. This became a lasting memory, and one which proved central in my spiritual growth and in determining my vocation in life.

In 1916 I was sent to St. Mark's preparatory school up in Massachusetts, and there it seemed natural for me to choose to go to Princeton to college. Some of my classmates went along with me, but before we left the school we had the great benefit of being exposed to the influence of an unusual headmaster, Dr. William Greenough Thayer, and his outstanding faculty. We were indeed already, for better or for worse, persons of privilege, if we had only realized it!

I began to consider whether or not I should go into the ministry and, in especial, prepare to devote my life to an educational ministry by teaching in a boarding school sponsored by the Episcopal church. There were many schools like Groton and St. Mark's and I realized newer ones were needed and would inevitably be created or spring up in areas where such a need was felt.

In 1920, it was on to Princeton, for I had been accepted there in the Class of 1924. And as early as the spring of my freshman year, I encountered the already famous person of Sam Shoemaker. Unlike many who resented Sam's direct approach and his eagerness to enlist younger men for the ministry, I welcomed his friendship and found it enriched me in a dozen ways. He had graduated from Princeton himself in 1916, so he was only seven or eight years older than I, and we found many common interests. I benefited greatly from his own experience at home and abroad.* In a "Religious Emphasis Week" for members of our class, Sam held meetings galore and made loads of opportunities to talk personally and privately with a whole batch of us. "The Oxford Group" was just beginning to be heard of and Sam meted out some central spiritual principles, which in that fellowship of Christians were being emphasized: (1) the priority of an uncompromising yielding of one's life to God; (2) the value of Bible study and unhurried time for private prayer and one's daily devotional life; (3) the possibility, nay the urgency, of interesting our own friends in the truths of the Spirit, and so on. It became engrossing, at times quite exciting, to realize how practical and practicable Christian faith could be, and I took to it, I suppose, like a duck to water.

*Sam Shoemaker had taught for a year at Peking University, where he had experienced conversion.

I early decided to make what Sam called a surrender of my life to God as revealed in Jesus Christ and to maintain a daily "quiet time" for meditation and guidance, and I felt strength and direction coming to me as a result.

After only three years in Princeton, I won a Rhodes Scholarship, and so it was that I transferred to Christ Church, Oxford. There I found the "Group" particularly strong and active. As a matter of fact, it was the life which other Rhodes Scholars had carried back to South Africa that brought about their name itself, given to these students by editors of the local press in Cape Town and Pretoria. I had some helpful contacts with the Group and kept in touch with them for several years. But it was another side of the Christian life on which I needed help. Let me explain this by a story:

One Christmas vacation I accompanied the Oxford University Ski (pronounced "shee"!) Club to Switzerland. We had a glorious time, but when I returned to Oxford my tutor, a learned scholar named the Reverend A. E. J. Rawlinson, asked me if I had made "my Christmas communion" in Switzerland. I had to admit that, in the informal, holiday atmosphere of the outing, I had not received Holy Communion. Then Dr. Rawlinson pointed out, in no uncertain terms, that the sacramental side of the Christian life was as essential as any other aspect of the Faith and should be scrupulously observed—especially by an aspirant for Holy Orders.

And so, at that point and in that way, I experienced a sort of conversion to the whole sacramental side of life in the church.

Actually, I spent three more years at Oxford University, studying theology. The life there was pleasant and I even enjoyed courses in philosophy and church history, as well as theology itself. But the question still remained as to what I should specifically do with my life after I returned home.

One afternoon I was out walking. Anyone who has walked across the fields near Oxford or through the meadows adjacent to Christ Church College will know what a refreshing and invigorating experience such a stroll can be. My walk took place in the midafternoon of a clear, bright day. When I came to a gentle stream I neither pursued it nor crossed over one of the convenient little bridges, but sat down on the grass for a half-hour, and there I had a vision, a vision of Christ. He seemed to be saying, "Be willing to stake more and more on me." And that settled it! I completed my theological studies, returned to the U.S.A., and joined the faculty of a brand-new boys' school at Lenox, Massachusetts. This was headed by the Reverend Gardner Monks, an old friend and one who had been a fellow student with me several years before at St. Mark's.

Also in Lenox I found that Trinity Parish offered me a well-rounded opportunity for worship and for service, and my spiritual life was speedily activated and deepened. Equally important at Trinity I discovered my wife, a lovely girl named Edith—Edith Minturn Bonsal, who happened to live just across the road from Lenox School. In due course Edith and I were married and in 1930 we moved to Middletown, Delaware, as I was fortunate enough to be called to be headmaster of another new school called St. Andrew's.

There we stayed and worked together straight along for twenty-seven years! We had three children, and we saw the school grow and prosper, and of course we made innumerable friends, both among the boys and their parents and also in Wilmington and in other parts of Delaware. My own evangelistic endeavors were encouraged by associates of Sam Shoemaker in New York and others, and we had many a visit from "teams" of Christians who were active in the new outreach of small laymen's groups and who spoke at the school.

When 1957 arrived—all too speedily—it was much too early to retire. I was thrown back, as at Oxford, on the direction of God Himself—or as some would call it, on the guidance of the Holy Spirit—and my wife and I were led to settle abroad, first in Singapore. We were not exactly missionaries nor was ours conventional missionary work, but we were under Anglican organizations and served Anglican-Episcopal congregations. This went on for about four years, and we worked successively at Saigon, Phnom Penh (Cambodia), and Vientiane (Laos). In various ways much happened to the glory of God and in the enlarging of His Kingdom.

Returning home again, we next settled in a wooded area between Elkton and Chesapeake City, Maryland, where we built a house, and for more than five years I was in charge of a revived parish in Chesapeake City. This was Augustine Parish, which had two parish churches but no resident rector.

My conversion extended over a number of years, and I thank the Lord for it.

The Night the Wind Blew—by **Wesley B. Ball***

A rare and wonderful combination of events and circumstances led to this special night with its strange pageant of events. The main ingredients or principal characters in the pageant were a country road, a tree, and—the wind.

I was in my sixteenth year in business. I was a claims investigator with the Canadian Pacific Railway and all its subsidiary interests. I loved my work, the trains, travel, and the adventure my work provided. Before I was thirty I had already worked much of the system; having started out in the Montreal office, I had been transferred to Toronto with special assignments in Sudbury, Ontario, where I was finally headquartered. From thence onto Winnipeg and out to the Saskatchewan office and then back to Montreal.

I had everything the world counted as success. It was a great feeling to leave the office with a briefcase full of files and move from town to city, investigating fatalities and accidents that resulted in law suits, or negotiate settlements with lawyers. There was power there as well as a sense of satisfaction when an investigation was completed and filed away.

But something was wrong. I couldn't quite put my finger on it. I was restless. I shared this sense of emptiness with my wife. Dorothy and I were happy. We had two lovely children and I knew it was only a short time until even greater things would come my way. I knew I was on the way to the top in my field.

*Wesley Ball is a minister with the United Church of Canada.

Occasionally when I was at my office in Montreal, I attended a noon church service for business people. This was short and to the point but very effective. But it always left me feeling worse than when I went in.

We were now living in the country about twenty-five miles from Montreal. Actually, it was my home village where I grew up as a boy. It was handy to my Montreal office and the territory I traveled in my work.

On that night when we were preparing for bed, the night the wind blew, I got dressed and told Dorothy I was going for a walk. I couldn't understand what was happening to me nor the vacuum I was carrying deep inside. It was about 1 A.M. and I came to a certain place in the road where suddenly a wind began to blow. Nothing unusual about that! Except it wasn't blowing anywhere else except where I happened to be standing. I saw that the tree to my left was actually bending over in the wind.

A strange fear got hold of me, and I started running down the road. I had never been afraid of anything in my life before. I ran until I could run no further, and that's when I heard a Voice. I have heard it many times since. I recognize it now and try to be obedient to it. It said, "If that's Jesus back there, go and meet Him."

Slowly I retraced my footsteps up the road to where the wind was blowing. I can't tell you how awkward I felt. This was absolutely stupid. Ridiculous! I had acquired a drinking habit but rarely drank to excess. This night I was in complete control but in a sense out of control. Running from the wind! Then came a Voice that whispered the name of Jesus.

When I reached a certain spot in the road (and I have been there many times since), the wind stopped and a peace came over me such as I had never experienced before. There are no words to describe it. Instinctively I knew I was in the Presence of God. I went down on my knees there in the road and prayed. I don't remember much of that prayer except that I blurted out something like: "Dear God, come into my life. If that's you who has been upsetting me then you must have a reason. I'll do what you want me to do."

Dorothy was up and waiting for me when I arrived home. She looked into my face and she said, "You have your answer." I didn't think it showed, but I sure felt it.

In the days that followed I thought that perhaps I was being called to be a Christian claims investigator. But as the months went by and Dorothy and I became involved in the church, I began to sense that God was calling me into the ministry. We talked about it and began to pray. Answers came quickly, and events all seemed to fall into place. It would take volumes to recount the next seven years, but suffice it to say that on the night of June 7, 1961, I was ordained into the Christian ministry in the United Church of Canada.

Since then, Jesus, Dorothy, and I have shared an adventure that makes anything I had ever experienced before pale into insignificance. I fail him but I try to be the best kind of pastor I can. I love Jesus with all my heart. The wind—I feel its gentle breeze. Sometimes it blows in strong gusts and at other times with a balmy, soft, spring gentleness. I know His name—He is the Holy Spirit.

Sometimes late at night, lying in bed, I hear a train whistle and a flood of memories sweeps over me and I begin to relive some of the experiences of those years. But when I listen, really listen, I hear the Wind sweeping past my window and unlike that fast freight moving through the night, I know where the Wind is coming from and where He will take me.

Not everyone experiences our God in this way. We must let God be God. But this was my experience, and I thank God for it.

All or Nothing—by Joyce Neville*

By way of background, let me say that I was brought up as an only child in a home where religion was *not* part of family life. I went to church and Sunday school now and then with friends of various denominations, and regularly for one year when I was eight years old and living with a Christian aunt and uncle. While attending college, I felt an urge to be baptized and join a church. I did not know why at the time, but years later my Christian grandmother mentioned that she always prayed for me. Knowing what I do now about prayer, I believe it was her prayers that drew me in that direction.

I went church-searching and attended an Episcopal church one Sunday. When the service was finished, I knew the Episcopal church was where I belonged. I felt I had come home. I loved the beautiful liturgy, the majestic music, the kneeling for prayers—everything. So I attended confirmation class and

---

* Adapted from *How to Share Your Faith Without Being Offensive* by Joyce Neville (New York: Seabury Press, 1979).

134

was baptized and confirmed. The class was extremely dull—church history and a lot of dry material—but I forced myself to go through with it. Looking back, I know the Lord was responsible for my faithful attendance.

To me, being baptized and confirmed was an intellectual exercise. Becoming a Christian was also an intellectual exercise. I decided, quite objectively, that I could accept the witness of the disciples and apostles, and therefore could accept Jesus as the Son of God. After my baptism and confirmation, I sighed with relief and told myself, "Now I'll go to heaven when I die!" I viewed baptism as a vaccination against hell. Christ was my Savior but not my Lord. I went to church only once a month for eleven o'clock Holy Communion because it made me feel good, although the sermons were dull.

My life went on unchanged. It had always been unhappy and chaotic, completely ruled by extremes of emotions dictated by what others did and said concerning me. Things went from bad to worse in the next seven years and I was really messed up in so many ways. By then I had graduated from college, had my own apartment and was working.

In August 1953, I decided I would commit suicide. I wasn't trying to be dramatic or get even with anyone. I just wanted out. I began putting all my affairs in order and very calmly planning the method.

The Tuesday night before the week-end I was going to do it, an Episcopal priest I knew, the Reverend Canon William O. Hanner, suddenly appeared at my door. I stared at him in surprise and, without even saying hello, exclaimed, "Father, what are you doing here?" He replied, "I just felt I should come to see you." (It was eighteen years later, while talking with a childhood friend, that I discovered she had called him, asking him to try to keep me from committing suicide, and he had kept her confidence. Since she claims to be a Jewish atheist, I asked her why she called the priest, and she replied, "Well, you wouldn't listen to me; I thought you might listen to a priest!")

Father Hanner came in and we talked. I told him I was going to commit suicide because life was not worth living. I asked him if I would go to hell. This was an academic question because the answer wasn't going to make any difference. He said that was for God to decide, and then he told me the thing that saved my soul, saved my life, and changed my life. He said, "Joyce, God has a plan for your life, and if you will surrender your life to Christ and ask Him for His blueprint for your life instead of giving Him your blueprint, you will find that life is worth living."

I had never heard anything like this before, and I replied, "But that's for ministers and missionaries, that's not for me."

Then we talked for an hour. I don't remember what was said except that I insisted I knew what would make me happy and would make life worth living, and that Father Hanner's idea wouldn't work for me. I remember that I was so adamant that he finally had to give up talking to me, and he said that if I decided to take his suggestion, I should contact him.

After he left, I thought it over a lot. I remember that I turned on the radio and it was playing, "You'll Never Walk Alone," and I thought that maybe God was trying to tell me something. I finally decided that

I had nothing to lose and, if the priest's idea didn't work, I could still commit suicide.

So I called Father Hanner and made an appointment to see him again right away. He suggested that I make a commitment in the form of sacramental confession. I didn't know how that could work since I felt every problem in my life and all my unhappiness were caused by others. Nothing was ever my fault. I was perfect, I thought. So I went home and, for the first time in my life, I asked God to show me what I had done wrong against Him and other people. Father Hanner had said to write it down. Well, I filled several pages in a steno notebook.

That weekend I came to confession. Father Hanner sat on the inside of the altar rail, and I knelt at the rail. I read aloud the confession form and all the things I had written down. However, I felt no real sense of guilt. It was strange. I knew I had done these things and I had to read the part that says I did them "by my own fault, by my own grievous fault," but I did not feel guilty—probably I was still subconsciously blaming everyone else.

Then, when Father Hanner pronounced the absolution, I suddenly realized what a sinner I had been. I suddenly felt a tremendous sense of guilt as I saw my life from Christ's point of view, and I began to see myself truly for the first time. But in the same instant it was all lifted from me—suddenly. It was a great mystical experience. It happened in an instant. Verses of Scripture that I had never understood flashed into my mind—"You must be born again" and "You shall know the truth and the truth shall make you free"—and I began to understand their

137

meaning. In the years since, the depth of my understanding of these and other Scriptures has increased many times over.

Then Father Hanner said that for penance I should say this prayer: "Jesus, I love you, help me to love you more. Jesus, I trust you, help me to trust you more." During the following years, I can't tell how many times I prayed that prayer, adding, "Jesus, I serve you, help me to serve you better," as He has given me ministries.

Then I stayed there alone a long time, praying. I said, "God, my life isn't worth anything to me. If it's worth anything to you, take it, it's yours, do whatever you want to with it." He knew I meant it.

While there, I asked the Lord—for the first time in my life—what *He* wanted *me* to do. It came to me strongly that I should move to Houston, Texas, with two girlfriends who had asked me to go with them but whom I had refused. I didn't know if this new spiritual life I had entered was real or if it would work, and I didn't know if I could survive without help, but I knew even at that early stage that, if this were real, then it should not, and could not, depend on the help of any person on a continuing basis. It had to be able finally to stand on its own.

In Houston, God gave me a whole new life that I never dreamed existed. After trying several Episcopal churches, I found St. Stephen's, where the Reverend Claxton Monro was rector. He also preached excellent sermons with real substance and was just beginning prayer groups, witnessing, practice of specific Christian disciplines, exercise of lay ministries, and other related activities, which have made this church such a powerhouse for Christ.

Without telling my whole story to him, I simply said that I had just given my life to Christ and asked, "Where do I go from here?" He put me into a weekly faith study and prayer fellowship group with six or eight other women, in which we discussed the Bible and many contemporary books on prayer, faith, Christian living, and spiritual healing. We talked about what God was doing in our daily lives and we prayed together spontaneously. Just from listening to them, I learned how to pray and got new insights into Scripture. I learned what God expected of me and what I could expect of Him.

One morning I awakened feeling great joy and great peace and great freedom. I was possessed by the realization that it was all true—everything I had been told was true! I accepted it not only intellectually and emotionally but spiritually, not only consciously but subconsciously. It was just there, never to leave. I felt that my life was full of the Holy Spirit. Oh, yes, I've had my ups and downs like everyone, but that morning I knew I was "over the hump." God had sent me to a church in which all I heard and experienced reinforced all I had been told.

CHAPTER FIFTEEN

Toward a Fuller Life

BY WILLIAM POPE

Aimlessness and dissatisfaction marked my life for several years. I was busy but restless.

After graduating from the university, I secured a job as a reporter. I had a vague idea I wanted to be a writer, but I found no deep satisfaction on a cub-reporter's beat. For a time I worked for a radio station, in the sales and advertising department, but after a lackluster few months I left.

Moving a thousand miles westward, I became employed as the young adult YMCA program secretary in one of Ontario's small but attractive cities. A change in external location, however, made little difference in my attitudes and motivations. I must have been a disappointment to my parents and to others interested in my career, as I wasn't settling down or focusing my energies in a purposeful way. Suddenly I received a shake-up in a surprising manner.

One Saturday night, while playing badminton, I received an eye injury. Early Sunday morning, a

The author is president of the Lancelot Press in Hantsport, Nova Scotia, Canada.

relatively successful operation was performed on my left eye. While considerable sight remained in that eye, there was nevertheless a distortion of vision that I had to learn to live with and that remains to the present day. I went home to recuperate and for several months had an opportunity for unhurried reflection and reading. Once again this time was largely wasted with trivial entertainments.

In my home city of Halifax I resumed work with the YMCA. In one of the mixed adult oil painting classes I had organized I became friendly with a young lady in that group. Isabel was stimulating and stable. She had a quick intelligence, and her views were often perceptive. She surprised me at times with her knowledge of the Gospels and with her spiritual insights. Looking back, persuading her to marry me was one of the most fortunate events of my life.

Still an inner restlessness persisted which seemed to reach a climax when we were expecting our first child. Again, I wanted to move into another occupation. At college I had been editor of the year book and had achieved some recognition for my efforts in that area. I had a lifelong interest in books and periodicals, so I decided to obtain a printing and publishing company. All the money we could scrape together was $5,000, and even in those days you didn't get much of a company for that sum.

It was at first not much more than a duplicaing firm in a rented, run-down building, but it was mine and I worked diligently. However, the machinery was deficient, almost obsolete, and I was inexperienced in all aspects of business. Despite my efforts, we lost money month after month. My dream

141

of producing beautiful books got no further than the printing of circulars and business cards.

Late one night, feeling frustrated and weary, I sat at a rickety little table in the shabby surroundings of my shop, engulfed in a faint but unpleasant smell of sewer gas! The place was dimly lit, but suddenly, in an instant, there came a soft illumination and with it a stillness that filled the room. And into my mind there flashed the thought that God was calling even me. Even me, with my record of work instability and failure, God was calling. He was calling me to a fuller life, a more meaningful life.

I hurried home to tell Isabel what had happened. "I think God is calling me into the ministry," I said finally. "Are you willing for me to become a theological student?" Fortunately she was encouraging and supportive.

In addition to my theological studies I ministered to a little congregation in Timberlea, Ontario, where we resided for two years. After ordination I served pastorates in both New Brunswick and Nova Scotia. In many ways I was growing in spiritual understanding. I wanted to grow, to be a finer person, to have my life count in a more meaningful way. However, I became restless again, dissatisfied to a degree, seeking for I knew not what.

At that time, I came to another crossroads. Some officials in the United Church of Canada came to me, suggesting that I head a committee that would establish a United Church home for the aged in central Nova Scotia. About a hundred churches would be involved in the financing of this project, and approvals would have to be obtained from seven different courts of the church. Several earlier attempts to get the home started had failed, but I was intrigued by this challenge—and I agreed to give it a try.

I sought out some of the most capable men and women in various churches, often those who had a business background, and these people became our first committee. We contacted architects and real estate people and formed tentative building plans. We went to church meetings with an enthusiastic proposal, but so much cold water was thrown on the idea that some wondered if the project could ever get off the ground. People had different ideas where the home should be located. Some felt there would be no financial support for it. And the church officials of the Maritime Conference in Sackville, New Brunswick, and the General Council in Toronto were not willing to give their approval to a project that did not have the support of local churches.

While formidable opposition was present, there were some people who thought a little progress was being made and that I was giving effective leadership. However, I had my own congregation to serve, and I wasn't able to travel sufficiently. I needed to visit the churches, talk with their ministers and other interested people, arrange for meetings, and in general seek support for the proposed home.

At this time I had a personal decision to make. I was offered a part-time job to promote the establishment of this home; I would be expected to devote at least one-half of my time to this cause, and I would be paid less than one-half of the salary I was receiving from my congregation. A second alternative opened when another small group came to see me. They were from a larger congregation, and they asked if I would

143

entertain a call from them to be their minister. This was an inviting prospect, an opportunity to serve in an enlarged sphere, and to secure a good, comfortable living for my growing family.

I struggled with this decision. I sought guidance from a few friends—and from God. Finally, although I didn't know how I could live on only half of what was a small salary, I decided to stay where I was and serve in what I considered a special ministry, the establishment of a church home for the aged.

My work was characterized by zeal. I sought out individuals and received support here and there. I talked with small groups; I spoke at Sunday church services; I invited church officials from Toronto to meet with our committee. After months of activity we still couldn't get the necessary approvals, but I was able to persuade four individuals to buy a lovely four-acre property and to hold this in trust for the church. We now had a distinguished and capable committee, a marvelous property to develop, and the determination to go ahead.

I threw myself into this work with abandon, counting not the hours spent nor the rebuffs received. I was in a tough struggle, and I enjoyed it. I spared not myself, but found satisfaction in furthering the cause. I was discovering the truth in what I consider to be one of the greatest statements in Scripture: "He that findeth his life shall lose it: and he that loseth his life for my sake shall find it" (Matt. 10:39).

Life had at last been taking on meaning for me, but I still had the problem of supporting myself and my family. I still had the desire to do something with books, to write or to publish them. While in the pastorate, I had written a little book entitled

Triumph of the Spirit, which Ryerson Press of Toronto published. Now, it seemed, I had the opportunity to do something further in this field. Despite my earlier, painful experience with a small printing business, I could never forget the exciting and constructive possibilities inherent in writing and publishing. I felt continually led in this direction and I had an inner urge that drove me irresistibly to this field.

A weekly newspaper and job printing plant became available, and for $50,000 I could be in business again. I spoke to a number of people and, believe it or not, they gave me financial support. Thus the Lancelot Press, Limited, was formed. But the venture got off to an unsuccessful start. I was not a newspaper man, and my interest was not in job printing. We lost money. There were times, after paying our six or seven employees, when there was no money left for my wife and me. We borrowed to the limit the bank would allow; each Friday we didn't know whether or not we would be able to meet the payroll. We were heading for bankruptcy.

No one wanted to buy the business, so one day, heavily in debt, I closed down our operation.

By this time the Windsor Elms, an attractive senior citizens home, had been built, and I was kept on as a part-time administrator with no salary increase. At the back of this property there was a large coach house, badly in need of repair, and not used for many years. I asked the directors of the home if I could use part of this building as a residence for my family and the other part as a publishing facility. After getting over their consternation at such a request, they finally agreed, and we moved in.

We fixed up the place as best we could, and Lancelot Press was *reborn*. We only had a few pieces of equipment and no employees outside the family. We were going to devote ourselves exclusively to book publishing, and we had one manuscript on hand—a book of sermons! This was the sort of material that is usually considered a slow seller, and I had not a candidate to rescue a floundering firm. But it was all we had, and we went ahead with all members of the family helping. The book was called *An Essential Greatness*, and we held a launching reception in the minister's church hall shortly before Christmas. We sent invitations not only to church officials and members but to the mayor and other city dignitaries. A former moderator of the United Church of Canada spoke during our introductory program, and the book was well and enthusiastically launched. Before the evening ended, hundreds of people purchased autographed copies, some for themselves, others for gifts. Soon a second printing was required, and the demand for the book held through four printings.

This was our first book, and from that point on we never looked back. Today we have over one hundred fifty volumes in circulation. New books came out slowly at first but now appear at the rate of fifteen to twenty a year, and the reprinting of successful titles forms the largest part of our business.

We publish books on a wide variety of subjects, although we have a special fondness for the strictly religious book. There are some books, however, regardless of their literary or commercial value, that we won't touch. For example, early on, we were offered a book of short stories by an English teacher. Some of these stories had won literary awards, but in our view they emphasized violence, meaningless violence, to an offensive degree. We said then, and we have not altered our minds since, that such stories were not for us. We have published sermons, prayers, religious books on various topics, biographies, histories, poetry, art, nature, and instructional books. All of these are positive and constructive in outlook.

The publishing of these books has provided us not only with a good living; it has enriched our lives immeasurably, in every conceivable way. A number of years ago we left the Windsor Elms, the church home on whose property we started book publishing. The home, in its own way, was performing a fine ministry, and support for its work was being received in many heart-warming ways. I vividly remember a call I received that informed me that our home was to receive a gift of one hundred thousand dollars. At about the same time a resident at the home died, leaving a similar amount in her will. These gifts encouraged the directors to expand and improve the facilities, to add an infirmary, and generally to upgrade the services offered. The home, firmly established, will be a blessing to many older folk for generations to come.

We moved Lancelot Press a few miles away, and it is now located on a thirty-five acre property, over-looking the Avon River outside of Hantsport, Nova Scotia. We have long since paid off *all* of our financial obligations, have purchased up-to-date equipment, and have established the firm on a reasonably solid financial basis. The *Atlantic Advocate*, a respected

Maritime magazine, said in a recent article that "Lancelot Press must be considered one of the most productive and successful of the little presses in Canada." They went on to discuss the range and quality of our books.

In a personal way, I feel, at long last, at home. The restlessness has gone. I have told friends on numerous occasions that I wouldn't want to change my place with anyone. I envy no one. I covet no other position and seek no other reward. I have my own small vineyard, and it offers me the opportunity and challenge for a full and satisfying life. Each day is fresh and exciting, with decisions to make and adventures to undertake.

My wife thinks I use the word *adventure* too frequently! I edited a book called *Adventures in the Holy Land.* I recently organized a spiritual retreat called the "Bermuda Adventure," and I am publishing a book for which I have suggested the title *Adventures of a Parish Priest.* Perhaps I *do* overuse the word, but I feel as if I were myself going from one adventure to another, with greater and more wonderful adventures still to come.

I am thankful my life is turning out as it is, but here I would like to stress that this has been *God's* doing. He has guided me from the beginning, and I have often been a reluctant follower. I have been impulsive. At other times I have been headstrong. I have turned from the vision God gave me, and His purpose for me, to follow my own will. Following this course always brings failure rather than fulfillment. But God has never given up on me. He has shown me, in a way that I cannot mistake, that a publishing business without a spiritual basis is not

His plan for me, and He has made it clear, also, that I can serve Him best, not in the pastorate but in a special ministry.

I am grateful for my theological training and for my experience in serving congregations, but I firmly believe God has led me to use this background in association with my publishing desires and experiences. To the extent I am doing this, I am convinced I am carrying out God's will for me.

I have come to this point in my spiritual journey, but I pray I may more fully do God's will in every aspect of my work, in every encounter with others, in all my relationships, be they with family, friends, associates, or strangers.

The Observer, the national United Church magazine, in a brief article referred to me as a "risk taker." I hope I merit this term—that I am willing to become vulnerable for good causes, to readily lose my life for His sake in order to continually find it, to be in the rich flow of creative and happy fellowship.

Complementing my work with Lancelot Press is the service I am able to render through the Second Mile Society. About ten years ago I asked a number of esteemed friends to join with me in founding this nonprofit society. Its purpose is to emphasize and promote constructive principles, spiritual values, and creative forces that enrich the life of people and society. We have attempted to carry out this purpose through the publishing of *The Second Mile* magazine, the distribution of religious books, the holding of public lectures, where renowned spiritual leaders are featured, and through the organizing of seminars and tours.

The Society is small compared to many organizations, but in its own way I feel it has produced some worthwhile fruit. That it is not greater in numbers or larger in influence does not unduly bother me. It is enough for me to know that, if I bring to it the best vision, energy, dedication, and resources I have—that is sufficient. If I grow, if I risk, if I become more capable, more open, sensitive, and obedient to divine guidance, then I firmly believe the work will be blessed in inconceivable ways. Three years ago, for instance, I would have been astounded if told that I was to organize and share in the leadership of groups that went on three major pilgrimages to various parts of the world, or would carry out a rededication service in the Holy Land on the Mount of Beatitudes. Now, other spiritual tours and services are being planned.

C. S. Lewis has said that most people are too easily satisfied, that God wants for them a fuller life than they are willing to accept. Through God's grace we are all given various talents, and about all we contribute to life is our faithfulness. When we use our talents faithfully, no matter how large or small they may be, we are invited into the joy of our Lord's fellowship.

This joy is enduring and wonderfully satisfying. Mother Theresa knows this joy as she ministers to some of the world's destitute people in their hour of need, some in their dying moments. Jean Vanier, himself brilliant of mind, experiences this joy as he serves the mentally retarded. This gracious invitation to enter the joy of the Lord is for all people.

I find the prayer of Ignatius Loyola beautiful and helpful:

Teach me, good Lord,
To serve Thee as Thou deservest;
To give and not to count the cost;
To fight and not to seek for rest;
To labor and not to ask for any reward save
    that of knowing that we do Thy will;
Through Jesus Christ our Lord. Amen.

I have gone a step on the spiritual road, but I still have a long, long way to travel. For I am, to a degree, a holdout. I shudder at risking all for God. Still God has touched my life. I am learning, maturing, and growing—grateful that each day, through work and worship, I am experiencing a fuller life.

BY SAMUEL M. SHOEMAKER

As a great Harvard psychologist once said, religion is always either a dull habit or an acute fever. For the lackluster, morally commonplace person, it is a dull habit if anything at all. For the person who truly enters into a religious experience, who begins living and acting as if God were real, it is an acute fever. It is not primarily an emotional experience, though it has emotion in it; it is the response of a man's whole self to God. It transforms one's whole existence; everything and everybody seem different because you yourself are different.

The doorway into the Christian experience and way of life is called conversion, a turning around, a new point of departure, a deeper quality of life.

Many readers will remember the New Testament story of Nicodemus, a high-minded, spiritually sincere leader among the Jews. In his talk with him Jesus said, "Except a man be born again, he cannot see the kingdom of God." Some of us may think that conversion is only meant for notoriously bad people, but Nicodemus was not a scoundrel or a rough-neck. He was the kind of a man who today might sit on a church board. But Jesus was not satisfied with him. He is never satisfied with half-way goodness.

Christian conversion has in it several elements. It has an *intellectual* element. One awakens to the fact that there are spiritual laws as operative and inexorable as physical laws, that there are sources of spiritual energy that may be drawn upon for daily life—which make of living a different thing. The Christian faith is not only a "way of life"; it is a belief, particularly one which focuses on the centrality and importance of Jesus Christ.

Then conversion has in it a *moral* element. Christianity answers the question of knowing what is right. True behavior is written on every page of the New Testament. Christ appears as judge of human practice and encourages one to put behind him, so far as he possibly can, whatever he realizes to be sinful.

Conversion also has a *psychological* element. In his great study, *The Varieties of Religious Experience,* William James traces the psychology of conversion with brilliant precision. When a profound change comes into a man's spirit it has effects which are psychologically recognizable. At the same time one must remember what another author, Harold Begbie, wrote many years ago in *Twice-Born Men* that, while psychology can explain religious experiences, it alone cannot cause them or bring them about.

There are two parts in a conversion experience: First there is *God's* part. Especially in the person of Jesus Christ, God sends out a standing invitation to the world to turn to Him. "Come home," He says; "come back to the Father of your spirits. Give up your self-will and accept my will for yourself—and you will find rest for your souls."

When we turn to Him in the first instance we are something like a naughty child who comes in to confess breaking a window. He expects punishment but may discover that his father is more hurt by it all than he is himself. As they talk things over they may decide not only that it will not happen again but that restitution will be made and the window paid for and the wrong righted. We never deserve to be so handled, but perhaps to our surprise we find we are. At the very moment when a sense of repentance becomes most acute, we become aware that a new chance is being offered to us, one mysteriously linked up with the person of Jesus. God forgives and further gives us a new life. That is His part.

Second there is *our* part. In many instances conversion never happens because an individual is unwilling to say yes to God, or is holding back something or several things which he is unwilling to give up.

Dwight L. Moody used to tell the story of a child who was trying to get a pebble out of a vase. He reached his hand in and doubled his fist around the pebble, and then could not pull it out. "Let go," said an older person standing by. The child dropped the pebble, the vase was turned over, and out came the pebble. Many of us need to follow that child's example and let go, for self-surrender is at the heart of our own experience of conversion. Thus God gives us a part, a free part, in our own conversion, and we express such freedom by asking God to take us, to touch us, and to guide us.

It was a great surprise to me to learn that I might have a part in my own conversion—in fact, that unless I wanted conversion enough to seek it by entire self-surrender, God would not thrust it on me.

Ask yourself what there is in your life of which God does not approve: Is there fear? lust? hatred? pity? despair? dishonesty? Or are you perhaps bound by several of these? You cannot be converted *around* these things. You must give them up to God in all abandon, and yourselves with them. Then something very fresh and very real will happen.